Feminine Ground:
Essays on Women and Tibet

Feminine Ground: Essays on Women and Tibet

Edited by Janice D. Willis

Snow Lion Publications
Ithaca, New York

Snow Lion Publications
P.O. Box 6483
Ithaca, New York 14851

First Edition USA 1989
Second Edition USA 1995

Printed in the USA

ISBN 1-55939-052-2

Library of Congress Cataloging-in-Publication Data

Feminine ground : essays on women and Tibet / [edited] by Janice D. Willis
p. cm.
ISBN 1-55939-052-2
1. Women in Buddhism—China—Tibet. 2. Women—China—Tibet. I. Willis, Janice Dean.
BQ7610.F45 1989
305.4'0951'5—dc19 88-39683
CIP

Contents

Karma Lekshe Tsomo

    Notes   135

    Contributors   165

Foreword

What you are now about to read represents a cooperative effort on the part of six Western women scholars to produce a volume of thoughtful, critical, and provocative essays regarding "Women and Tibet." Certain decisions regarding the project were made by us early and sanctioned unanimously. We decided, for example, *not* to limit ourselves—either with respect to specific areas, time periods, or methodologies. We neither wanted this work to be solely devoted to women and Buddhism (recognizing that other religious traditions were, and remain, practiced by Tibetans), nor limited to a particular time frame (recognizing the value of contemporary accounts as well as ancient ones; and of oral traditions as well as written ones). Neither did we want to restrict ourselves solely to religious literature to the neglect of the secular. (Though most of the present essays look at religious texts drawn primarily from Buddhist sources, secular literature is not forgotten. See, for example, Gyatso's use of historical documents; and Aziz's injunction to incorporate more ordinary lay biographies and autobiographies into our investigations.) Lastly, we did not want to speak only of women *in* Tibet but rather, to discuss broader issues regarding Tibetan ideas *about* women, the female, and the feminine. The result is a collection of extremely thoughtful essays on diverse, though related, subjects which we hope will be instructive and enjoyable—the true sense of *edifying*.

The reader will find a variety of methodologies represented here, for the individual authors of these essays have expertise in the history of religions, in anthropology, and in philosophy. A diversity of approaches is also evidenced. Hagiographical, philosophical, hermeneutical, mythological, and anthropological discussions will be found here. All of the contributors are scholars of Tibet, trained in its language (as well as in Sanskrit). Moreover, all are conversant with and concerned about contemporary issues of feminism.

The first of the essays presented here—that by Rita Gross—focuses upon the eighth century Tibetan *yoginī*, Yeshe Tsogyel (Ye-śes-mtsho-rgyal). Rita Gross approaches the life of Yeshe Tsogyel as hagiography and uses the text "in the way the hagiography traditionally functions—as inspiration to the student practitioners who look to the great teachers as role models." Thus she discusses its ability to inspire us as women (and men) today. In the course of doing so, she presents a provocative analysis of Tsogyel's "relational life"; one which judges the great *yoginī* to exemplify an enlightened approach to "relationships," successfully integrating relationship and spiritual discipline. Gross suggests that "Tsogyel's and Padmasambhava's essential complementarity and equality also provides a model of a female-male relationship. . ." and that the Vajrayāna presents "a balance of feminine and masculine energy. . .on the ultimate. . .and on the empirical level." Lastly, she challenges feminists to use Tsogyel's example as a model capable of helping to transform both contemporary Buddhism and feminism.

Janet Gyatso's essay (and to some extent, my own) tackles the use of feminine symbolism. One could say that we both go back in *time*, to discuss space. For Gyatso, that space is more particularly "ground"—as this has been described and regarded by Tibetan mythology and by individual Tibetans themselves. What Gyatso attempts to show is that the land of Tibet, the very ground itself, has since ancient times been regarded as a demoness, an ancient *Srin-mo*. Having suggested that the "ground" of Tibet has been regarded by some as being synonymous with the feminine, a demoness, and with the older indigenous religious traditions, Gyatso then draws out some of the implications of this idea, especially as it relates to the manner of Buddhism's establishment there.

Clearly, all of us have been fascinated by the exemplary women practitioners whose lives are recorded and narrated in the scriptures of Tibetan Buddhism. As a contribution to the present volume, Miranda Shaw translated from the Tibetan an "ecstatic song" composed by Lakṣmīṅkarā, one of the four women among the famed group of eighty-four Indian *mahāsiddha-s*.

In the piece on *ḍākinī*, I take the opportunity to review, and to speculate on, the seeming plethora of diverse views regarding this immensely important tantric symbol and idea. While *ḍākinīs* have certainly been known to take on women's bodies, my chief concern is with "her" meaning as this relates to Buddhist tantric theory and practice generally. Because I see the symbol as one indicating, and indeed enjoining, "complementarity," I see obvious connections between some of my conclusions and some of those voiced by Rita Gross.

Having discussed ancient religious models—as these relate to particular women and to general ideas regarding the feminine in Tibetan sources, the collection next turns to what may be called a more contemporary, sociological, view of Tibetan women. Barbara Aziz prepares the groundwork for this with her piece, "Towards a Sociology of Tibet." Aziz would have us begin such a study with an analysis of Tibetan women. And, to address the issue of the social reality of women, Aziz begins most interestingly by looking at the *language* used in reference to them. From this simple but provocative point, she then moves to detailing the various dynamics and relations of Tibetan women's work—especially as this is exemplified in a modern-day hotel setting in Lhasa. Aziz's study also suggests the importance of secular—especially biographical and autobiographical—literature for providing us with adequate and accurate pictures of the Tibetan woman's social world. Through such portraits we may get a better (and certainly, a fuller) picture of Tibetan society as a whole.

Following Dr. Aziz's essay come two pieces which focus on Tibetan nuns. My own essay, "Tibetan *Ani-s*; The Nun's Life in Tibet," is intended both as a challenge to the overly idyllic and idealized picture of Buddhist monastic life fostered by early Western travellers and their "capital-centered view" of Tibet's monastic institutions; and as a counterbalance which aims at indicating the variety and flexibility of the forms of religious practice actually observed in Tibet, especially as these relate to the practices of five twentieth century Tibetan nuns.

The concluding essay, by Karma Lekshe Tsomo, not only informs us about such issues as the current status of the nun's ordination in Tibetan Buddhism, but also provides us with a descriptive analysis of a number of contemporary Tibetan nunneries in India and Nepal.

Two years have gone by since this project was first begun. I have learned a lot from my part in it. It is my hope that the reader will likewise profit from it.

1. *Yeshe Tsogyel: Enlightened Consort, Great Teacher, Female Role Model*

Rita M. Gross

Recently, two English translations of Yeshe Tsogyel's biography have been published.[1] They constitute an important resource for those interested in Tibetan Vajrayāna Buddhism who do not read Tibetan. Yeshe Tsogyel, probably Tibet's most influential and famous female religious teacher and one of the world's most significant female religious exemplars, lived in the eighth century C. E. An important teacher in her own right, she was also, in her early life, the student of Padmasambhava as well as one of his principal consorts until he left Tibet. Padmasambhava is a semi-legendary figure, the first great tantric master to come from India to Tibet to teach Vajrayāna Buddhism.

This text is so provocative and intriguing that scholars and theologians with many interests can profitably study it, thereby enriching their reflections and their scholarship. I come to this text as an historian of religions, a feminist theologian, and a practitioner of Vajrayāna Buddhism. I am primarily interested in the text as hagiography and I will be using it in the way the hagiography traditionally functions—as inspiration to student practitioners who look to the great teachers as role models.

However, many of my concerns and conclusions are not traditional.

The text is both difficult and provocative. Despite many years of the study and practice of Tibetan Buddhism, I often found the text difficult because of the inevitable Vajrayāna technical language that preserves the inner secrets of the oral tradition while revealing the outer level of information. If this text is difficult for someone with some access to Vajrayāna oral tradition, I do not know what it would be like for someone with little knowledge, especially practical knowledge, of Tibetan Vajrayāna Buddhism. At times, when Tsogyel's various practices and initiations are described, the text may read to an outsider like the book of Leviticus. On the other hand, in terms of the sheer story line I have never read a similar story and find it quite fascinating.

Anyone familiar with the basic mythic outline of the hero's life[2] and with the life of Siddhārtha Gautama and other great Buddhist exemplars will immediately recognize that Tsogyel's life-story manifests those patterns. In addition, the biography is characterized by a strong element of the kind of sacred history typical of Tibetan historical writing. In sacred history the story is told from the point of view of enlightenment and narrates the emergence of primordially enlightened mind into phenomenal reality. Thus many events in Tsogyel's biography are told on two levels—on a "mythic" level narrating the life of a great human religious teacher and on the level of "sacred history" narrating how enlightenment manifested in the form of Tsogyel. These two forms of the story can seem far apart and the "sacred history" is often based on esoteric concepts.[3]

Tsogyel's biography is divided into eight chapters. Their titles, paraphrased or quoted from Tarthang Tulku's translation, summarize well her life history. (1) "Yeshe Tsogyel sees that the time has come for her to teach and appear in the world"—which narrates, on the esoteric level, the story of her conception. (2) "The arrival and manifestation of Yeshe Tsogyel in the land of Tibet"—which narrates Tsogyel's exoteric human conception and birth. (3) "Yeshe Tsogyel recognizes the impermanence of all things and relies upon a teacher"—which narrates Tsogyel's failed attempts to avoid conventional marriage, her suffering within conventional marriage, and her eventual union with her guru, Padmasambhava. (4) "Yeshe Tsogyel asks her teacher for instruction in the Dharma"—which narrates Tsogyel's early training and her acquisition, by buying him out of slavery, of a principal consort, Atsara Sale. (5) "The manner in which Tsogyel did her practices"—which narrates Tsogyel's solitary three-year practice in a cave at the snow line of a Himalayan mountain, the incredible austerity and discipline of those years, and the sexual and other fantasies that were part of her experience in those years. (6) "A summary of the auspicious signs which occurred as Yeshe Tsogyel practiced and the siddhis she manifested after achieving realization." (7) "The manner in which Yeshe Tsogyel acted to benefit sentient beings"—which narrates Tsogyel's enlightened compassionate activities throughout her life. Finally, (8) "How Yeshe Tsogyel reached her goal, achieved Buddhahood and entered the expanse of all that is."[4] Out of the wealth of her story I have chosen to focus here on Tsogyel's relational life, especially focusing on how her relational life intersects with her practice and her eventual achievement of enlightenment and Buddhahood. Initially I had thought I would focus only on her relationships as consort, but I found her relationships with women so interesting that I also want to include them in my discussion.

In my reading, the single most dominant theme in the story of Tsogyel's relational life is the single-mindedness with which relationships are seen, not as ends in themselves, but as aids or detriments on the path of practice to Tsogyel's eventual realization of Buddhahood. When Tsogyel is portrayed as consort to Padmasambhava the emphasis is on how the relationship fosters her spiritual training and development, not on their hypothetical erotic relationship or on how she meets Padmasambhava's needs. Similarly her relationships with various other consorts foster her own spiritual development as well as theirs. They are not primarily erotic encounters to meet quasi-instinctual needs. The consort-relationship develops both partners in their spirituality which, though no different from ordinary physical existence, nevertheless pushes people beyond conventional habitual patterns into luminous awareness of the sacredness inherent in ordinary experience. Her relationships with women were similarly oriented to practice and realization. Tsogyel is seen either as the discoverer and teacher of talented female practitioners or a sister-adept of other highly developed women. In several episodes of her biography Tsogyel and other female adepts meet, share teachings with one another, and delight in each other's *dharmic* company.

This overarching theme in Tsogyel's relational life is foreshadowed already in the esoteric story of her conception—"Tsogyel saw the need for beings to be taught and manifested in the world."[5] Seen from the viewpoint of enlightenment narrated in sacred history, Tsogyel is a multilayered being. Her *Dharmakāya* manifestation is Samantabhadrī—primordial Buddhahood; her *Saṃbhogakāya* manifestation is Vajrayoginī—one of the most important *yi dam-s* (personal, non-theistic deities) of Tibet; in the *Nirmāṇakāya*, the apparition-body of ordinary human form, she is Yeshe Tsogyel, eighth century Tibetan woman, great teacher, enlightened consort.[6] Seen from the other side, this Tibetan woman who exerted herself on the path of practice and attained Buddhahood in a single lifetime manifests the inherent *Saṃbhogakāya* and *Dharmakāya* qualities of all beings and all experience. To appreciate Tsogyel's life, it is necessary always to read and hear the story on many levels at once, especially on the levels of both myth and sacred history.

According to the narrative of her prehistory, Tsogyel, as a lady-merchant appeared before a previous Buddha and expressed her vow never to be reborn except to benefit beings. Eventually she became the (Hindu) Goddess Gangā, revered Śākyamuni Buddha and became the (Hindu) Goddess Sarasvatī. Then, according to the text, Padmasambhava reflected, "Now is the time for the Goddess Sarasvatī to manifest and help me spread the Mantrayāna teachings,"[7] which led to

Tsogyel's human conception and birth. At the same time, on another level, her *Saṃbhogakāya* level, Tsogyel is quintessentially understood as the speech emanation of Vajravārāhī (a slightly more esoteric form of Vajrayoginī). Vajravārāhī, like most *guru-s* and *yi dam-s*, takes five emanations: body, speech, mind, quality and action. Padmasambhava, who "worked through appropriate and mystic consorts in order to spread the Mantrayāna doctrine,"[8] had consorts who were emanations of each of these five aspects of Vajravārāhī. In addition, there was a sixth "essence *ḍākinī*" who was also an important consort, as well as "...appropriate and mystic consorts more numerous than the sesame seeds it would take to fill the four walls of a house."[9] Tsogyel is the speech emanation and one of two major consorts. Some of the other consorts are important in the unfolding of Tsogyel's relational life-history.

Having seen the need for Tsogyel's manifestation in the world, the *guru* and *ḍākinī* (Padmasambhava and Tsogyel in supramundane form) meet in supramundane realms to engender Tsogyel. The story of her conception is told on two levels. On one level, "the vajra of the *Yab* joined the Lotus of the *Yum* and together they entered the state of great equanimity...The Great Bliss of the *Yab-Yum* penetrated everywhere into all realms of the world, and great tremors and earthquakes shook the universe. Light rays burst forth like shooting stars from the union of the *Yab* and *Yum*. The red letter A came into view, and from it spiralled a garland of white vowels. The white letter *VAM* appeared and from it spiralled a chain of red consonants. The lights and letters penetrated into the world, striking the ground...in Tibet."[10] Meanwhile, on another level, "One day when the Prince, my father, was twenty-five years old, while he and his queen, my mother, were enjoying the pleasures of love-making, my mother had a vision."[11] Extraordinary visions continued throughout the night for both. Nine months later the queen gave birth painlessly to a female baby with unusual abilities. Almost immediately, it was predicted that either she would become a great religious teacher or the consort of an emperor, an obvious parallel to the Buddha's life story.

Despite this extraordinary conception and birth, as is typical of many mythic biographies, the parents had absolutely no appreciation for her extraordinary potentialities and were concerned primarily with making a proper marriage for Tsogyel. This marriage was very difficult to arrange because Tsogyel's mundane beauty aroused intense jealousy between the mundane kings. Finally her parents simply sent her away, with the edict that whatever man caught her first could have her and no one else could wage war over that event. Tsogyel's desire not to enter such a marriage was not taken into account by anyone. When captured, she resisted to the extent that her feet sank into a boulder as if it were mud and only after being whipped "until my back was a bloody pulp,"[12] did she submit. However, she kept her resolution to obtain enlightenment in a single life and escaped while her captors celebrated her capture in a drunken stupor. Living in a cave, subsisting on fruit, she was found out, and the wars over her threatened to continue. To end the turmoil, the emperor took Tsogyel as wife. The other suitors had to submit and soon thereafter, the emperor, who was eager to learn the Buddhist teachings, gave Tsogyel to the *guru* as part of his *maṇḍala*-offering.

This turn of events suited Tsogyel perfectly, since she cared only to learn the teachings and her *guru* was willing to teach her. However, she did not receive the full teachings at this point. Her *guru* consort, Padmasambhava, told her "...without a consort, a partner of skillful means, there is no way that you can experience the mysteries of Tantra... So go to the valley of Nepal where there is a sixteen-year-old youth with a mole on his right breast...find him and make him your ally."[13] She found her consort, after a long harrowing journey, but she found him in slavery and had to purchase his freedom. She did so by raising from the dead the son of an important Nepali family. They paid her with gold, which she used to purchase the freedom of her consort. Soon thereafter Tsogyel matured her practice with a three-year solitary retreat at the snowline. Well into the retreat, among the many illusions she found it necessary to experience were projections of:

> charming youths, handsome, with fine complexions, smelling sweetly, glowing with desire, strong and capable, young men at whom a girl need only glance to feel excited. They would begin by addressing me respectfully, but they soon became familiar, relating obscene stories and making lewd suggestions. Sometimes they would play games with me: gradually they would expose their sexual organs, whispering, "Would you like this, sweetheart?" and "Would you like to milk me, darling?"...all the time...trying all kinds of seductive foreplay. Overcome by the splendour of my *samādhi*, some of them vanished immediately; some I reduced to petty frauds by insight into all appearances as illusion;...."[14]

However, during later stages of her practice, she practiced "the last austerity practiced for my own benefit. ...The austerity of the 'seed-essence of coincident Pleasure and Emptiness'" with three consorts including the redeemed slave.[15] Very soon after completing this practice, she returned to her *guru* Padmasambhava. He praised her dharmic accomplishments lavishly and extensively after saying:

> O *yoginī* who has mastered the Tantra,
> The human body is the basis of the accomplishment of wisdom
> And the gross bodies of men and women are equally suited.
> But if a woman has strong aspiration, she has higher potential.[16]

After this point the narrative focuses more on Tsogyel's accomplishments and her activities to benefit others, though she continues further advanced practices as well. Immediately after Padmasambhava had praised her accomplishments and made the above comments about female practitioners, he suggested that she find a certain youth who would be her consort in the Yoga of Immortality Practice. She replied that she also wanted the initiation of Vajrakīlaya or Dorje Phurba, the Remover of Obstacles, specifically because of obstacles from the outside world that she, a woman, faced.

> Inadequate women like me with little energy and an inferior birth incur the whole world's hostility. When we go begging the dogs are hostile. If we possess food or wealth then thieves molest us. If we are attractive we are bothered by fornicators. If we work hard the country people are hostile. Even if we do nothing the tongues of malicious gossips turn against us. If our attitude is improper then the whole world is hostile. Whatever we do, the lot of a woman on the path is a miserable one. To maintain our practice is virtually impossible, and even to stay alive is very difficult.[17]

After receiving the Vajrakīlaya initiation, she quickly found the required new consort and together they quickly "achieved identity with Dorje Phurba,. . .had a vision of the deities of Phurba's *maṇḍala* and gained Phurba's *siddhi*."[18]

We are now at the last two chapters of Tsogyel's biography concerning her activities in "establishing, spreading, and perpetuating the teaching" and her "fruition and Buddhahood." She gains innumerable disciples, both female and male, and brings many of them to high levels of realization. She also leaves many *terma*[19] texts in various places to be rediscovered later, when the time is ripe. These activities occurred both while she was with Padmasambhava and after his departure, when she remained behind, "because of her superiority to work for the welfare of beings and to fill the earth with the Guru's teaching."[20]

After Padmasambhava's death she performed her final austerity " 'the exchange of my *karma* for that of others' "[21] in which she took on or worked with the extreme sufferings of others. She extricated from hell an official who previously had given her extreme trouble. She says, "I gave my body to ravenous carnivores, I fed the hungry, I clothed the destitute and cold, I gave medicine to the sick, I gave wealth to the poverty stricken, I gave refuge to the forlorn and I gave my sexual parts to the lustful. In short, to benefit others I gave my body and life."[22] In this phase of her practice, two especially difficult challenges came to her. She chose to accept both of them without being coerced in any way. She gave her body-parts to another person to be used in a transplant operation. She also lived as wife with an extremely repulsive, diseased man who cried out for companionship.

After these accomplishments she began to manifest throughout the universe in different forms satisfying whatever were people's needs—food, wealth, clothing, etc. "To the childless I appeared as sons or daughters, bringing them happiness; to men desiring women I appeared as attractive girls, bringing them happiness; to women desiring husbands I appeared as handsome men, bringing them happiness."[23] The list continues, dealing with those afflicted by anxiety and frustration, those wandering in the *bardo*,[24] in short to those in every difficult situation. She explains, "In short wheresoever is sentient life, there are the five elements; wheresoever are the five elements there is space; insofar as my compassion is coextensive with space, it pervades all human emotion. Appearing first as one emanation and then as another, I remained. . . for twelve years."[25]

Immediately thereupon the narrative concludes with Tsogyel's death. Yeshe Tsogyel "composed [her] self in the *samādhi* that brings all things to extinction."[26] In a long concluding narrative her students ask for further teachings and receive final teachings and predictions.

> With this farewell she ended, and light, shimmering, sparkling iridescently in splendid vivid colours, streamed towards the South-West and vanished from sight. All of us who witnessed this final departure prostrated countless times after her. . . . Then our minds full of grief, our hearts heavy, our stomachs in our mouths, our tears flooding the path, staggering, una-

> ble to control our bodies, panting and heaving, we retreated to the meditation cave. . .where we spent the night.[27]

Before going on to comment on these facets of her story, I want to narrate briefly several more incidents exemplifying other variants of the relational theme.

Not all of Yeshe Tsogyel's relationships with men are "positive," at least in the conventional sense. What is notable about these episodes is the way they are turned into *dharmic* events by Tsogyel, promoting either her own practice, or the realization of her very tormentors. The first negative episode involves her attempts to avoid conventional marriage and the cruel treatment she receives from her captors. But she transforms this into her first lesson in basic *dharma*, concerning the pervasiveness of suffering and impermanence. A predharmic initiatory ordeal necessary to motivate one towards the path of *dharmic* practice and an important event in any Buddhist biography. After she meets Padmasambhava she says,

> I am young, but not inexperienced
> For suffering was revealed to me at the age of twelve
> When my parents denied me my request for celibacy
> And gave me as a bride in a lay marriage.[28]

And he replies, confirming her assessment of her experience.

> You, a woman of sixteen years,
> Have seen the suffering of an eighty-year-old hag.
> Know your pain to be age-old *karma*,
> And that the residue of that *karma* is erased.[29]

Because of this coincidence of her suffering and her meeting the teacher, she is able to hear and practice Buddhism and the Vajrayāna.

Two other events stand out. While on her journey to the Nepal valley to find her consort Atsara Sale, seven thieves sought unsuccessfully to steal her gold.[30] Many years later, after completing most of her practices, including the Vajrakīlaya practice for removing obstacles, she was robbed and raped by seven bandits.[31] In both cases, her speech to her tormentors converted them to the path of *dharma* and transmuted their energies from their previously aggressive and unenlightened expression to *dharmic*, enlightened pursuits. In all fourteen cases the formerly depraved men became her students when she unlocked for them some insights into the sources of their destructive energies and how to work with those energies more effectively. I find these examples quite provocative and challenging.

Finally, in terms of biographical episodes, I want to present a few examples of Tsogyel's relationships with women. In the narrative, she has many, many women students, of whom a few stand out. One of them was thirteen when she began to bring offerings to Tsogyel during Tsogyel's three-year retreat. Tsogyel asked the girl's father, a Bhutanese king, to allow the girl to accompany her, which he agreed to do. The girl, named Tashi Chidren, became the Activity Emanation of Vajravārāhī and one of Padmasambhava's six main consorts. She was with Tsogyel until the end, one of her eleven root disciples. Another of Tsogyel's eleven root disciples, with her until the end, was Kālasiddhī, who became Tsogyel's disciple much later. She also was recognized as an emanation of Vajravārāhī, the Quality Emanation, and became one of the six major consorts. Among the eleven root disciples are also two other women, one of the queens, Liza Jangchub Dronma, and Shelkar Dorje Tsomo. (Incidentally, faithful Atsara Sale, the redeemed slave, was also there at Tsogyel's death.)

More extended discussions of Tsogyel's companionship with the other two women, who are major emanations of Vajravārāhī, are given. Early in her practice, just after meeting Atsara Sale, they go to visit Śakya Dema, the Mind Emanation of Vajravārāhī. At that point Śakya Dema is probably more accomplished than Tsogyel, who asks Śakya Dema for teachings. Śakya Dema then asks Tsogyel to give her any teachings she can pass on. The two women also acknowledge each other as consorts of the *guru*. "Then our finite minds united in the Buddha's mind and we exchanged precepts and instructions."[32] Near the end of her life, in the last story narrated before Tsogyel's last instructions and prophecies, ". . . the flower Mandāravā came from India. Emerging from the sky with her six disciples, she greeted me. She stayed with me for thirty-nine human days and we exchanged and tightened our precepts, making endless discussions on the dharma."[33] Mandāravā was the Body Emanation of Vajravārāhī and major consort of Padmasambhava in India. The two women exchanged advanced teachings with each other and wrote encomiums to one another. Both expressed their unity with one another and resolved to work to enlighten all sentient beings. Mandāravā ends her poem to Tsogyel thus:

> May I be one with you, Mistress of Powerful Magic.
> Hereafter, purity suffusing the sphere of purity
> In your field of lotus-light,
> You and I will project emanations of Buddha's *karma*
> As light-forms of Guru Pema Skull-Garland's compassion:
> May we empty the depths of the three realms of *saṃsāra*.[34]

To conclude the condensation of Tsogyel's relational biography, I quote a passage describing her essential relationship with Padmasambhava, her root *guru* and her consort.

> The Guru and Ḍākinī, mystic partners, having identical ambitions, serve all beings with skillful means and perfect insight; with the same activity of speech we expound *sūtras* and *tantras*; with the same apparitional projections we control the phenomenal world; with the same knowledge and talents we work for the good of the teaching and all living beings; with the same karmic activity we utilize the four *karmas* of transformation at will. Ultimately Pema Jungne and Yeshe Tsogyel are identical to [*Yab-Yum* of the Absolute]: our Body, Speech, Mind, Activity, and Quality are coextensive with all-pervasive space.[35]

This account of Tsogyel's relationships is haunting, provocative and appealing to me. I know of no similar story of a woman whose relational life and spiritual journey are so intertwined and support each other so thoroughly. I would like to sort out several themes important to that assessment.

First, a sharp differentiation exists between conventional relationships and *dharmic* relationships, relationships between *sangha* members on the path. Tsogyel bitterly fights against conventional marriage and suffers greatly within it. Many other times, including the two encounters with thieves discussed earlier, she encounters aggression, violence, and attempts to restrain her from her spiritual practice by malicious or misguided outsiders. These attacks are based on the neurotic passions or *kleśa-s*, rather than on the englightened passions, or mindfulness practice, and on compassion. Tsogyel, because of her high spiritual attainments, provides a model in working skillfully with these situations, and transforming difficult circumstances into spiritual practice, both for herself and often for her tormentors as well. Bringing such difficulties into one's spiritual practice rather than merely freaking out by launching into a major outburst of neurotic passion is a very important practice and skill in Vajrayāna Buddhism.

Dharmic relationships are different. Not based on neurotic or unenlightened passions, they are neither mutually exploitative nor exploitative of one or the other of the partners. Regardless of who is the leading or more developed partner, the relationship serves to develop both partners more fully, to mature them both in spiritual practice. Though one partner may be the more advanced practitioner, that person's practice still needs the support of the less developed consort. Tsogyel's consorts are often referred to as her "supports," as are Padmasambhava's consorts. Furthermore, these roles are not gender-fixed; they depend on levels of development. Padmasambhava is Tsogyel's *guru*; she is his consort during periods of training. But she is also *guru* to both female and male students; some of the male students are also her consorts supporting her practice.

In the long run, Vajrayāna Buddhism presents a balance of feminine and masculine energy, both on the ultimate level and on the empirical level.[36] During the period of development and training to achieve that ultimate balance, sometimes the leading role is taken by a man, sometimes by a woman. When such status or authority is devoted to enlightening all beings rather than to aggrandizing one's own position, exploitation cannot happen. Thus the power-plays so common in conventional relationships are not present in Tsogyel's *dharmic* relationships. And the neurotically compulsive insanity that so often plagues relationships is not part of Tsogyel's relationships with her *dharmic* consorts and friends.

This rather different quality of relationship comes through especially clearly in the unconventional and non-possessive conduct of the relationships. Though Tsogyel is Padmasambhava's consort, she is not with him much of the time. Often she is doing solitary practice or is practicing with her other consorts. When she is with him, the narrative concerns the practices they did together and their activities to teach and spread the *dharma*. Tsogyel's other consorts became Padmasambhava's students and attendants; her female students sometimes become Padmasambhava's consorts. Various combinations of these *dharmic* friends often travel and practice together. Furthermore, Tsogyel's most vibrant encounters with women occur with Padmasambhava's other major consorts, Śakya Dema and Mandāravā, her equals on the path.

An aspect of this non-possessive and non-neurotic mode of relationship involves the way sexuality is integrated into these relationships. They are not primarily erotic encounters; they are primarily *dharmic* encounters to which there seems to be a sexual aspect. In fact, the sexual level of these relationships is so much *not* the focus of the narrative that I bring up the topic at all only because of stereotypes about the Vajrayāna and the importance of consorts in some aspects of Vajrayāna Buddhism. This is not because Tsogyel's sexuality is ignored or repressed; working out an enlightened version of her sexuality was apparently an important part of Tsogyel's training during her retreat. In that narrative her sexual fantasies—still based somewhat on wantingness, desire, and ego orientation—are dealt with very explicitly. I found the passage quite interesting both because it reverses the more usual motif of women tempting men and because, as far as I know, spiritual biographies of women usually do not portray the women as having strong sexual desires themselves, but mainly as having to fend off the lust of men.

It is interesting that the most explicit discussion of Tsogyel's sexuality involves her inner world. As many feminists have pointed out, such an inner life usually is based on rejection of aspects of one's own psyche, which are then projected onto others, turning them into objects. Those objects then become, in terms of Buddhist psychology, the objects of desire, grasping, and fixation, and the whole cycle of *saṃsāric* suffering is kept spinning. When Tsogyel has integrated her psyche, has become more realized, men are not such objects of grasping and fixation. Then all aspects of experience, including sexuality, are in proper relationship with one another, a situation which cannot happen when sexuality is an end in itself, engaged in with an ego-orientation of self-gratification and clinging. When sexuality no longer involves a process of objectification, it does not demand special comment or description. Tsogyel's integration of spirituality and sexuality provides an important paradigm for understanding the proper connection between relationship and *dharma* practice. This topic is important for contemporary women, because *dharma*, in the extended sense of concern for truth and social service are often difficult for women to integrate with their conventional role expectations and their natural longing for companionship.

What is the connection between relationship and spiritual or intellectual discipline? Which one is or should be the leading element in one's life? Which one promotes which? What mishandling or unbalancing of the two would cause destruction of one or both? These are important questions, especially because so frequently relationship is the most difficult and frustrating arena of life, much more so than one's livelihood, profession, or spiritual practice. This occurs because of unbalanced priorities and unrealistic expectations of relationship as the solution to existential anxiety and suffering. What Tsogyel's relational biography shows is that relationships carried on in the context of a spiritual discipline can dissolve clinging, grasping and fixation and need not involve the anxiety, neurotic passion, and jealousy of conventional relationships. So often in conventional relationships, expectations, needs and neurotic passions cause the relationship to increase rather than to ease suffering. The only way out of this situation is to dissolve the unrealistic expectations surrounding the relationship. These ego-fixations and ego-orientations dissolve through spiritual discipline. Tsogyel's "vision-quest"[37] all her life was to dissolve the confusion and clinging in her mind, not to find the relationship that would make her feel better. Her biography demonstrates a proper balance or prioritization of relationship and spiritual practice. She seeks enlightenment and gains both enlightenment and enlightened relationships.

In her ability to integrate enlightenment with enlightened relationships, Tsogyel provides a provocative, challenging and untypical model for women and companions of women. Tsogyel, in her relational life, is consort, not wife and not nun. In order to undo the fixations of conventional relationships it is not necessary for her to renounce relationship; in this combining of relationship and *dharmic* achievements she presents a significant model in my view. As consort, she provides an unusual model contrasting to the much more typical Buddhist roles for women as either wife or nun. The consort model, as exemplified by Tsogyel, is very inspiring despite its rarity and unconventionality, particularly for contemporary women whose vision-quest is enlightenment and *dharmic* service. In many ways, this model is much more workable than either of the conventional models—wife or nun. Conventionally, at least in patriarchal societies (and all Buddhist societies have been patriarchal), wives are essentially servants to their husbands and children. It is not a role that fundamentally promotes realization, though many women manage to circumvent the liabilities of the role. On the other hand, male companionship, heterosexual experience and the presence of male energy, are important to some women as a component of the total path of spiritual discipline they tread. The nun role, despite its liberating potential, does not allow this kind of male companionship. Tsogyel as consort, though unusual in the repertoire of roles for women found in Buddhist literature, is worthy of emulation by, and inspiring to, contemporary women.

Particularly noteworthy and exemplary about Tsogyel's role as consort are the non-monogamous and non-possessive nature of her relationships combined with her ability to be a companion to her consorts while not losing her vision of her own reason to live—enlightenment and service. This model is inspiring and comforting to women; it is also challenging to companions of women. Not only are women called upon and challenged to become a Yeshe Tsogyel; their companions are challenged to become a Padmasambhava, willing to engage in an intense relationship with a woman without the safety of monogamy, either on her part or his, or the subservience of the wife-role in patriarchal society.

Tsogyel's and Padmasambhava's essential complementarity and equality also provides a model of female-male relationship far more appropriate than the conventional patriarchal model of male superiority or the separatist and female supremacist version of current feminist theory. I began this study of Tsogyel's biography curious about whether her story indicated the existence of any traits, qualifications, or dilemmas that are intrinsic to women on the spiritual path and not shared by men. To answer this question adequately it would be necessary to compare Tsogyel's biography carefully with other biographies in the same genre.[38] Since I have not yet conducted this study to my satisfaction, my speculations are preliminary, possibly subject to change. However, at this point, my conclusion is that Tsogyel's biography, compared with biographies of other similar spiritual heroes in Vajrayāna Buddhism, does not point to essential, basic differences based on gender that affect or enhance one's spiritual practice, though some more superficial differences probably occur.

Two statements, one from Padmasambhava and one from Tsogyel, on this question are found almost side by side. Both have already been quoted. After Tsogyel's completion of her three year retreat, her guru says:

> The human body is the basis of the accomplishment of wisdom
> And the gross bodies of men and women are equally suited
> But if a woman has strong aspiration, she has the higher potential.[39]

A few paragraphs later, Tsogyel complains:

> Inadequate women like me with little energy and an inferior birth incur the whole world's hostility. When we go begging the dogs are hostile. If we possess food or wealth then thieves molest us. If we are attractive we are bothered by fornicators. If we work hard the country people are hostile. Even if we do nothing at all the tongues of malicious gossips turn against us. If our attitude is improper then the whole world is hostile. Whatever we do the life of a woman on the path is a miserable one. To maintain our practice is virtually impossible and even to stay alive is very difficult.[40]

Probably she is exaggerating because she is making her case to receive the Vajrakīlaya—Remover of Obstacles—practice. The more obstacles, the more need for the practice, since in Vajrayāna Buddhism one must always justify receiving a new practice rather than demanding it or simply beginning to do it.

It is interesting that both Tsogyel and Padmasambhava attribute the better situation to the other sex, though Padmasambhava does not dwell on the difficulties of the male role. Such cross-sex curiosity and jealousy is actually very common in the literatures of many disciplines and cultures. Such comments probably indicate that everyone recognizes superficial differences between women and men and one often feels that she or he is missing something. Superficially, whichever sex one is, there are some disadvantages and some advantages, and one *is* missing something because one can be only one gender.

Nevertheless, spiritual biographies like Tsogyel's seem to me to emphasize that these differences are rather unimportant on any absolute or ultimate level, though certain ways of giving social form to these differences can be completely unjustifiable and cruel. On the path of spiritual discipline, women and men face the same essential difficulties of overcoming conventional lifestyles. Men too must often circumvent parental pressure to marry and continue the family enterprise. They must equally overcome neurotic passions such as aggression, ignorance, clinging, pride or jealousy.[41] They equally experience discouragement, resistance, and many other such obstacles intrinsic to spiritual practice. The portrayals of enlightened, compassionate activity also betray no essentially different activities. Both teach, debate, discover students, give initiations, practice, edit and compose texts, and travel about the country giving whatever help is needed. And there is no evidence that the enlightened state of mind, the mind of Buddha, is different in a male than a female body. In fact, it is self-contradictory to imagine that One Mind could be different in different bodies—leading to the common statement that Enlightenment occurs neither in a male body nor in a female body. Gender is not a category that is of ultimate significance.

This conclusion, if correct, is important since it is contradictory not only to conventional patriarchal thought including those strands of Buddhist thought which state that womanhood is an inferior birth,[42] but also to some currents in contemporary feminist thought, which posit an intrinsic female superiority based on female body experience and/or states of mind.[43] This separatist feminist train of thought has been produced by an over-valuation of the relative uniqueness of women's experience. The conventional generic masculine, which sometimes treated women as men and sometimes as nonexistent, is certainly inaccurate; therefore all the literature exploring women's experience is a needed corrective.[44] However, this correcting balance does not require a conclusion of innate essential differences between women and men with its consequent claims for the intrinsic moral superiority of women. Recognizing and exorcizing the evils of patriarchy does not depend on defining women as innately and essentially biophilic while men are necrophilic.[45] In fact, this conclusion and the essential impetus of feminism toward an enlightened society[46] are incompatible with each other. If the sexes are that innately different, if sexual and moral dualism is that deep, there is no hope for humanity and it makes little difference which gender is theorized to have the "right" attitudes and values. If roughly half the human species is unhuman, lacking in basic goodness, how would we ever have an enlightened society?

My conclusion, of course, raises as many questions as it answers. If women and men are *not* so different, why have sex roles and stereotypes been so dominant, and so often so patriarchal and advantageous to men? In this context, I do not wish to explore historical and cross-cultural answers to that question, but to bring the question back to Tsogyel's biography and to Tsogyel as role model. Is Tsogyel a token, so rare as to be worthless as a role model? Worse, is Tsogyel's experience so much like that of other great spiritual models, many of whom are men, because, essentially she is one of the few women in a male system, a male-identified woman?

A positive answer to the latter question would, I believe, depend on a prior philosophy of feminism with which I do not agree. Therefore, I would not interpret Tsogyel as a male-identified woman. The former question, about Tsogyel as token because of the imbalance between numbers of women and men of her calibre is much more significant, disturbing and provocative. If women and men are equally suited for enlightenment, why are there so few women like Tsogyel relative to the numbers of men like her?

Actually, for the time and place described in the text, I was surprised to have the opposite reaction: there were a lot of women like her! Four of her eleven root disciples were women and the text constantly narrates her interactions with female students, both laywomen and nuns. Things seem to have become more male-dominated later. We may be seeing another of the "first generation phenomenon," so familiar to women's studies.[47]

Actually, when we ask whether Tsogyel can be a role model because she is a token, we are not asking whether Tsogyel can be a role model, but whether Tsogyel's *society* can be a model society. The presumed negative answer may be depressing in some ways, but it is not determinative of anything and should not be given too much importance. "There are no fully adequate models in the past" has become a slogan for feminism. That slogan has been used to liberate from past authority; it has also been used as an expression of poverty mentality or frustration with the past. I would suggest more a sense of "there *could be* no fully adequate models in the past." I believe technological conditions prohibited fully adequate models in the past. But on a deeper level, an adequate model in the past would be useless if not realized and actualized in the present. It would even cease to be a model if it were only past; it would become a memory or a dogma. But if one is seeking to realize and actualize the present moment, the present situation, then one has an adequate model somewhere, somehow. Models are much more our inspiration than they are something that once existed separate from us.

Still, the "numbers question" has troubled me for many years and has been my most serious misgiving about and feminist criticism of Buddhism. I have questioned where in Buddhist thought or institutions would lie the explanations. It is not found in the basic and essential Buddhist thought or worldview, which is profoundly non-dualist and therefore non-misogynist. A genderized deity, gender heirarchy, and hierarchial dualism simply are not characteristic of core Buddhadharma, at least as expressed in the Mahāyāna and the Vajrayāna; and the feminist Buddhist critique requires different categories of explanation than does the feminist Christian critique.[48]

Currently, I am exploring an explanatory *nexus* of institutions, *karma*, and social reform, both to explain the past and as a wedge for contemporary challenge to change. Briefly put, though the Buddhist worldview is exemplary, classical Buddhist institutions are not. Furthermore, I am suggesting that a certain interpretation of the notion of *karma* prevented the rise of social criticism and social reform as a dominant Buddhist issue. (This is, I believe, a subtly mistaken view of *karma*, but it is impossible to discuss the issue fully in this context.) Therefore, Buddhists did not notice the contradiction between their non-misogynist worldview and their patriarchal institutions. Rather they explained that everyone's situation, including women's relative difficulties and even their female gender was due to their *karma*. Under then prevailing conditions, empirically women's lives were harder than men's and, empirically, it was more difficult for women to practice. That much was conceded, even appreciated. Unfortunately this situation was then explained as due to the *karma* of the beings currently reborn as women, rather than to social institutions in need of reform. Given the severe demands of intensive agriculture, high infant mortality rates, limited life expectancy, and lack of birth control, it may have seemed more reasonable to attribute the harshness of women's lives to *karma* than to imagine that humans could control or change those conditions. However, those conditions do not prevail today; therefore the institutions' social roles and life plans that coped with those conditions are out of date. The *karma* of women's lives has changed drastically, so that there are no adequate models in the past. Thus, rather than discouraging social criticism and social reform, an understanding of *karma* promotes it. Institutions must change in order to accommodate the drastically changed possibilities of women's lives. There are no adequate models in the past, including Tsogyel's society. But Tsogyel herself, enlightened consort and great teacher, remains a greatly inspiring female role model.

2. *Down With the Demoness: Reflections on a Feminine Ground in Tibet*

Janet Gyatso

> For they give satisfaction to one another and make reparation for their injustice.
>
> —Anaximander, frag. Bl(DK)

"Land of the Bad Ones"[1]; "Land of the Red-faced Flesh-eating Demons";[2] "Tibet, Land of the Hungry Spirits."[3] These epithets reflect what seems to be an ancient conception of the country of Tibet as being filled with spirits, mostly malevolent, that needed to be appeased and controlled in a complex variety of ritual ways. Such concerns are attested in some of the earliest Tibetan documents available. But not only do the Tibetans refer to the animistic character of their religion in such epithets; they are simultaneously expressing a proclivity to characterize themselves, or at least their ancestors, the human inhabitants of Tibet, and indeed the basic nature of their national race, as being savage, uncivilized and demonic. The Tibetans themselves are the "red-faced flesh-eaters,"[4] the denizens of "the little-known country of barbarous Tibet."[5]

If we can believe the contemporary Chinese court historians, this demonic character was not entirely figurative. The Sui and T'ang dynasty annals know the Tibetans as ruthless and aggressive, traits that were not unrelated to Tibet's success in the military sphere in its early historical period, particularly in China in the eighth century, A.D. The Tibetans had, according to the *T'ang shu*, (and notwithstanding some exaggeration about "barbaric" neighbors),

> hundreds of thousands of men ready to bear arms. . . .They prize physical strength and despise old age. A mother salutes her son, and a son has precedence over his father. . . .They prize death in battle and hate to end their lives by sickness. . . . When someone is defeated in battle or runs away, they fix a fox-tail to his head to show that he is cowardly like the fox. A great crowd will assemble and he is certain to be put to death.[6]

And in the *Sui shu*, "They are all warriors. . . .They are given to lechery and obscenity to an extent unknown even among any other savage race."[7]

This preponderance of aggressive, male values notwithstanding, there is reason to suspect that in some Central Asian societies at this time the *female* also partook of such virtues, or at least was influential and powerful. We have evidence of an amazonian-like Land of the Women, perhaps two of them, in areas bordering Tibet, from both Chinese and Indian sources.[8] A society that may have been Tibetan is described in the *Sui shu* and the *T'ang shu* as being matriarchal and matrilineal. The supreme ruler was the queen, and sons took the family name of their mother. The men were still the warriors, but they were directed by women, who "do not esteem highly the men, and rich ones have always men servants who arrange their hair. . ."[9] Erik Haarh, in his extensive study of the central Tibetan Yar-lung dynasty, also notes an importance of certain female deities in early theogonies. He traces a "genitrix" back through the dGe-lugs-pa protectress dPal-ldan

Lha-mo, to a variety of pre-Buddhist female deities including Srid pa'i rgyal mo, mother of nine primordial eggs; A phyi gnam gyi gung rgyal; and the ancient sPu yul mo btsun gung rgyal, "progenitrix" of the *Yang-bsang-lugs* rendition of the origin of the Tibetan kings.[10] Haarh finds especially significant the importance of the queen's family in the royal succession. Matriliny is also suggested in a Tibetan text of aphorisms from Tun-huang that may be connected to a female-dominated society of the fifth century Sum-pa people; here is voiced the sentiment that "the woman who is the good wife severs the husband's lineage."[11]

Returning to the nonhuman world, it is certainly the case that the hordes of malevolent beings that populate the Tibetan imagination and undermine the noble aims of humanity are not limited in gender to the masculine. There are numerous types of such evil spirits, and each class has both male and female members. These spirits are sometimes conceived hierarchically, especially when recounted in creation myths as progenitors of the Tibetan people, but the hierarchies and relationships vary widely, as do the precise character and ritual function attributed to each type of spirit. In the words of Snellgrove and Richardson, "it has long since become impossible to distinguish between them."[12] In any case, it is specifically the female gender of one of the demon species, the *Srin*, that comes to represent both the spirit world in its entirety, and the demonic nature of the early Tibetans, in a founding myth concerning the Buddhist domination over the indigenous Tibetan religion.

The *Srin* are a particularly fierce evil spirit. They were later identified for translation purposes with the Indian *rākṣasa*.[13] But they are clearly ancient and indigenously Tibetan. They are to be found in many origin myths[14], and are often affiliated with specific regions of Tibet[15]. In its explicitly female form, the *Srin-mo* is cast in one source as the giver of catapult and infantry[16]. A bKa'-brgyud text knows the principal Srin-mo demoness as Frog-head Bloody-eye (sBal mgo khrag mig).[17] In an early Tun-huang text many other *Srin-mo-s* are named.[18] Later said to have been subdued by Padmasambhava at Rong rong lung pa nag po,[19] *Srin-mo-s* are placed in the retinue of such wrathful Buddhist deities as dPal ldan lha mo,[20] Rahu,[21] and lCam sring, in a group called the "male and female Srin of the four times."[22]

In the traditional Buddhist recounting of Srong btsan sgam po's introduction of that Indian religion into Tibet, it is this female *Srin-mo* who is particularly resistant to the new faith, and who is posed as one of its major obstacles. The very land of Tibet as a whole is seen as being constituted by the vast supine body of a *Srin-mo* demoness, here unnamed. This country-wide being must be brought under control before Buddhism can be established in the country. Her domination precedes by several generations the capitulation *en masse* of the manifold Tibetan spirits to the superior power of Padmasambhava, who bound them all by oath to become *dharma* protectors.

Like much of what we are told of the introduction of Buddhism into Tibet, the story of the supine *Srin-mo* does not appear in the scanty contemporary sources that have survived. The earliest known version of the story comes rather from the recast, mythologized accounts of the events of the Yar-lung dynasty, accounts that date from the second period of the propagation of Buddhism in Tibet (*phyi-dar*), after the tenth century. Michael Aris identifies the twelveth century *Maṇi bka' 'bum*, the seminal *gter-ma* text for the Buddhist retrospective account of King Srong btsan sgam po's reign, as the first appearance of the supine demoness.[23] However, there are echoes of the story in the *sBa bzhed*, a text that was revised in the same period as when the *Maṇi bka' 'bum* was written, but the core of which is a contemporary account of the eighth century Khri srong lde btsan's period.[24]

In any event, it is not my purpose here to determine the origin or antiquity of the supine *Srin-mo* story as such. Rather, given its pervasive presence in virtually all Tibetan histories of the period in which it is placed,[25] I would like to reflect upon the story's significance. In particular, who is this demoness and why is she female? What elements of the Tibetan world at the time of Buddhism's entry does she represent? What is the fate of that world at the hands of the Buddhist narrative?

1. THE SUPINE DEMONESS
(*Srin-mo Gan-rkyal-du bsGyel-ba*)

As the *Maṇi bka' 'bum* tells the story, the *Srin-mo* is perceived first by the Srong btsan's betrothed, the Chinese princess Kong jo. The princess is consulting her geomantical charts to determine why she is encountering so much difficulty in transporting a statue of Śākyamuni to the Tibetan court. Dramatically, the magnitude of the problem and its implications, not only for the importation of the Buddha image but also for the very fate of Buddhism in Tibet, dawns on Kong jo as she interprets the results of her calculations. In this passage from the *Maṇi bka' 'bum*, the anthropomorphic vision of the country of Tibet-as-demoness presents itself to Kong jo as she shifts her focus from the particular circumstance of the statue-bearing chariot getting stuck in the mud, to the significance of the large scale configurations in the lay of the land itself:

> Kong jo understood that this Snow Land country (Tibet) as a whole is like a Srin-mo demoness lying on her back. She understood that this Plain of Milk of Lha-sa is a palace of the king of the *Klu*. She understood that the lake in the Plain of Milk is the heart-blood of the demoness. The three mountains surrounding the Plain of Milk are the demoness's two breasts and her life-line (*srog-brtsa*). The eastern mountain promontory afflicts the west; the western afflicts the east; the southern afflicts the north; the northern afflicts the south.[26]

Thus is the entire shape of the landscape perceived as highly deleterious. The account goes on to attribute the unsavory behaviour of the country's inhabitants, such as banditry, etc., to the *Srin-mo*-land. However, the imaginative analogical perception engendered by the geomantical calculation also suggests positive images latent in the Tibetan topography:

> Of the four directions of this place, in the east is a mountain like a heap of flowers. In the south is a mountain like a heap of jewels. In the west is a mountain like a stack of *stūpas*. In the north is a mountain like a conch-shell cup on top of a tripod. If you build a chapel on the Plain of Milk[27], the naturally [auspicious] qualities of Tibet will come to develop.[28]

There follows a complex set of instructions to counteract the many inauspicious configurations in the Tibetan land and to make possible the building of the Jo-khang chapel. Particularly called for is a transforming of certain sites seen as "faults" in the landscape—i.e., spots inhabited by the indigenous Tibetan spirits, such as the palace of the *Klu*, the camp of the *'Dre*, the bed of the *Ma mo*—into sites suitable for the congregation of the king's subjects, monks and mendicants. This includes a filling in of the lake in the Plain of Milk, and the establishment of Kong jo's Śākyamuni image in "the center of the land, in order to suppress the *Klu* palace."[29]

What finally emerges as that which will conclusively bring the demoness-Tibetan-land into submission is the construction of edifices, specifically Buddhist chapels, at certain key spots (*me-btsa*) in the country.[30] The king, perceiving that the demoness is waving her arms and legs, determines that by placing edifices on her land-body, she will be physically pressed down (*gnon*) and pinned, with her arms and legs immobilized. The buildings on her shoulders and hips will suppress the four main sectors (*ru-chen-po bzhi*); those on her knees and elbows will control the four borders (*mtha'-'dul*); those on her hands and feet, the four further borders (*yang-'dul*). Thus is articulated an elaborate scheme of thirteen Buddhist temples, with the Jo-khang poised on her heart, and with three concentric squares encompassing the Tibetan map: the center, the inner realm, the borders, and the borders beyond.[31] The temples are then erected (some of which, as Aris has shown, are still standing today in Bhutan). "And through the power of all the Buddhas and Bodhisattvas, the Venerable Avalokiteśvara made a Dharma palace in Tibet, and thus saw to it that what would benefit the Land of Snows was accomplished."[32]

2.

It is a violent conception indeed: a ferocious demoness as the land upon which stand the architectural structures of the normally pacific tradition of Buddhism, structures that here suppress and dominate. The story's provenance is indisputably Buddhist, and it postdates the events it describes by several centuries. But it not only preserves the Buddhist version of the manner in which Tibet became a Buddhist country; there are telling traces here of Tibet's shadowy archaic religion, at least of how it was, and still is, viewed by Tibetans, Buddhist tampering notwithstanding. Moreover, even in its adulterated, tampered form, the saga of Tibet's conversion to Buddhism betrays a complex set of links with patterns of thought known in many parts of the world, links which can tell us something about the nature of that early, elusive phase of Tibetan religion itself.

Thinking of this demoness-land, one is put in mind first, of course, of the perception of the primary stuff of the planet—the *Ursache*—as a living being. Such a being is perceived throughout the world at the dawn of humanity, and is most often conceived as feminine—Mother Earth (although there are some notable exceptions, as in ancient Egypt where the god Geb is the earth and his feminine counterpart Nut is the sky). In her supine position, the Tibetan giantess is especially reminiscent of a world-supporting tortoise spoken of in various parts of Asia, usually portrayed as feminine, and which at least according to the Buriats is also turned on her back, with the world built upon her stomach.[33]

But unlike the Greek *Gaia*, this Tibetan Mother Earth is not beneficient or sustaining. Just the opposite, the supine demoness threatens to undermine goodness, advancement and civilization in Tibet. In this role, the *Srin-mo* demoness belongs to a particular subtype of the world-being image, which occurs in certain creation narratives. Although her story is, strictly speaking, not a creation myth—a long succession of Tibetan kings and other figures and events precedes the episode in both history and myth—for the Buddhists the introduction of the *dharma* in Tibet does mark a creation of sorts, the dawn of civilization, and the institution of order, in a previously untamed and savage land.

The creation narratives to which the *Srin-mo* story is akin begin with a pre-existing primordial chaos, a chaos which is a female being. Then the female chaos is conquered, and she becomes the stuff of which the world is fashioned. Naturally wild and dangerous, when controlled it is just she out of whom civilization is built. A seminal creation myth exemplifying this syndrome is that of the Babylonian Tiamat, goddess of the monstrous deep. Tiamat is slain, quartered and measured out by the god Marduk, who uses the parts of her body to make heaven and earth.[34] Her eyes bring forth the Tigris and Euphrates rivers; her breasts become the hills.

Both the Tiamat and the *Srin-mo* narratives share an element seen not uncommonly in Near Eastern and Indo-European mythology, namely, that particular parts of a divine or primal body come to constitute particular parts of a newly created place. Sometimes this reassignment is marked by a dismemberment. We know the theme well from the poignant *Purāṇic* story of Satī, consort of Śiva. When she died and the bereaved god carried her body on his back in mourning, the other gods relieved his burden by causing her body to break into parts and fall to the ground. The spots in India where the parts of her body struck the ground became the sacred pilgrimage spots of Hinduism—particularly the place where her *yoni* landed.[35] Less well known, but probably in some sense informing the *Srin-mo* story, is a Tibetan creation myth from the non-Buddhist Klu-'bum cycle. Here the body of a *Klu-mo*, serpentine being from the deep, again female, gives rise to the parts of the world: her head becomes the sky; her right eye the moon, her left eye the sun, her teeth the planets, her voice thunder, her breath clouds, her veins rivers.[36]

Not all partitioned primal bodies are female. Ymir, the primordial Germanic male giant formed from coagulated ice, is slain and dismembered by his grandsons. His skull also becomes the vault of heaven, and his flesh becomes the earth, his bones the mountains, his blood the ocean.[37] Another primal man, Puruṣa, is often commemorated to the south of Tibet, in Indic mythology, as Prajāpati. His dismemberment facilitates the formation of societal order, the Indian castes, as well as the seasons, and the parts of the world: his head becomes the sky, his eye the sun, etc.[38]

Partition, demarcation and order: the structural theme of these various myths aptly conveys the act of the institution of civilization. We know that for the Tibetans the theme of dismemberment infuses myth and ritual from an early date.[39] Moreover, the image of quartering is central to the conception of Tibetan polity as early as the "four corners" (*ru-bzhi*) in Tibet's military organization.[40] Clearly, the series of concentric squares depicted in the image of the *Srin-mo*, segregating the inner areas of Tibet and delineating the outer realms of the barbarians, has a related societal import. As Aris has shown, the ethnocentric cast of the inner, outer, and barbarians-beyond structure probably has Chinese origins[41]. Nonetheless, the intimations of political domination and organization do not sufficiently explain the myth of the supine demoness, and certainly not its significance for the introduction of the Buddhist religion. Moreover, there remains as a central element in the *Srin-mo* image a basic perception of the earth and the forces it embodies, forces that have deepest significance at the level of personal and spiritual experience of the world.

3.

It is striking to note that the narrative of the supine demoness does not record her conclusive slaying or decisive finishing off.

There is no mention of her death resulting from her horizontal crucifixion. Quite the contrary, there are important ways in which the demoness remains very much alive, a question to which we will return below.

Despite the other affinities with the creation myths noted above, the *Srin-mo* story differs in the important respect that she is not, in fact, actually dismembered. Various parts of her body do constitute the various regions of Tibet, but these parts are never severed from the whole in order for that constituting to take place. Rather, the parts of her body are merely held down (*gnon*). Unlike Prajāpati, who only comes to be reassembled in man's ritual construction of the *agnicayana* altar[42], we wonder whether the demoness's unity has ever been sacrificed at all.

Thus, the primary operative element in the domination of the *Srin-mo* may more precisely be said to be the set of chapels that pin her down. The image calls to mind another theme from world mythology, where pins and other, often large, vertical devices function not so much to destroy, as to hold and transfix. In the Vedic myth of the Indrakīla, the nail driven into the head of the serpent Vṛtra does not slay the serpent but rather stabilizes him. The nail also serves to prop up the sky.[43] This line of thinking engaged the early Tibetans as well. Mountains were thought of as "sky pillars" (*gnam-gyi ka-ba*) or "earth nails" (*sa-yi phur-ba*).[44] Man-made pillars called "long stone" (*rdo-ring*) were erected by the early Buddhist kings to mark possession of the spot and domination of the underworld below. King Khri srong lde btsan's tomb has a pillar called "fixing peg."[45] Another earth-nail pillar is at bSam-yas Monastery.[46] A related "peg that transfixes the earth" is an integral part of building rituals in Southeast Asia.[47] John Irwin writes of the "pillar cult" in both Indic and Judeo-Christian traditions.[48] In Chinese mythology, the Goddess Nü-kua also fixes the world by cutting off the feet of a turtle (cousin of the supine tortoise of the Buriats?) and uses them as pillars to separate earth from sky.[49] And in Tantric Buddhism, the act of demarcating, building and transfixing are brought together in the *Mahāvairocana* rites for constructing *maṇḍalas*, where the pins that lay out the structure also "pacify the site."[50]

And so the *Srin-mo* is not slain by the temple/nails, although she is surely held immobile. But even this immobility is not the only aim. What is thereby allowed is also of key importance. The temples built by Srong btsan sgam po simultaneously suppress the sites of the *Ma mos* and *Klus* on her body, and transform those places into Buddhist realms. Similarly did Apollo slay Pytho—"the bloated she-dragon"—and by that very act take full possession of the sacred Delphi.[51] Again, it is a common pattern: the old site of the indigenous religion is associated with some sort of special configuration in the land, in which the powers of the deep are perceived as having particular force. It is a place connected with spirits, spirits that course in a cavernous underground realm, and are often of a female nature or associated with some overarchingly feminine flavor of spirituality. The incoming religion seeks out those very sites, and builds right on top of them. The new structures obliterate the old places of worship, but gain instant history and sacred power thereby.

Part and parcel of the relationship between the demoness land and the architectural structures upon her seem to be certain sexual innuendos. If the *Srin-mo* is a Mother Earth, then the architectural structures that hold her down must be seen as overtly masculine. At one point in the *Srin-mo* myth this is quite explicit: one of the pinning structures is a Śiva *linga*, to be set on the "earth-enemy" (*sa-dgra*) in the east, a place which is "like the Srin-mo's pubic hair."[52] Vertical buildings, imposing structures. . .erections; in contrast, the feminine earth is associated with fertility, nurturing, receptivity—even the stereotype of weakness and vulnerability voiced in Aris's reading of our *Srin-mo* as "the ancient yet virgin territory waiting to be subjugated and civilized."[53] The very horizontalness of the ground itself is significant; as the feminist Irigaray sees it, the ground is the "matter upon which he will ever and again return to plant his foot in order to spring further, leap higher."[54] The vertical and horizontal axes themselves come to have a value judgement inherently associated with them. Consider the moral connotation of "uprightness" in English, which may be compared with the lowly status of that which is "base."[55]

4.

Why does Buddhism, upon entering Tibet, find the feminine ground to be monstrous, chaotic and inherently evil? Buddhism also portrays the Tibetan national character as female, and dangerous, in another story, this time concerning the origin of the Tibetan race itself. It is a commonly repeated tale: The Bodhisattva Avalokiteśvara, incarnated as a monkey, is enjoying a life of solitude in the mountains, when he is lured into marriage by a desperate, insistent rock demoness. Their offspring become the first Tibetans. Yes, this lusty female is also called *Srin-mo*, and the *Maṇi bka' 'bum*, in a passage separate from the tale of her embodiment of the Tibetan land, explicitly attributes the source of the love of killing, physical strength, and courage, all typically Tibetan traits, to this demonic ancestress. The more lofty virtues of spirituality and compassion, also seen to be embedded deep in the Tibetan character, are traced to the paternal monkey.[56]

These gender-specific assignments of personality traits can be linked with a tendency in certain early Buddhist canonical texts, noted in recent years by Diana Paul and others, to portray women as the source of desire and attachment, primary enemies of the celibate Buddhist meditator-monk.[57] Later, Mahāyāna Buddhism compensated for this bias by reasserting the irrelevance of gender to the spiritual path and in enlightenment. Indeed, Tantric Buddhism, so prevalent in Tibet, may privilege the female[58]. Yet the general Tibetan image of women, as in the word itself, *skyes-dman*, lit., "inferior birth," retains some of the old suspicions and bias.[59]

A connection between the feminine, evil, and the *Srin* class of spirits is not unknown to Tibetans independent of Buddhism. Such an equation is made as early as an account, from the sixth century, of the sKyi Kingdom. In this account, the ascendency of women, linked to such qualities as their coming to be "ungentle," is a result of the decline of civilization, attributed to the power of the *Srin*.[60] A cluster of negative qualities is also assigned to woman/*Srin-mo* in the Bon-po epic *gZer-myig*. At one point, the father and brother of gShen rab's mother complain,

> That which is called woman (*bud-myed*) is the demoness (*srin-mo*) of action. Because her grounding in attachment is so great, she is to be considered a ghost (*'dre*). Because her grasping lust is so strong, she is the cause of the world of the womb.[61]

But the domination of our supine *Srin-mo* has a more profound meaning than the simple-minded misogyny of statements such as these. For one thing, the *Srin-mo* does not primarily represent woman, but rather a religion, or more accurately, a religious culture and world view that is being dominated.[62] And so we need to consider the nature of that pre-Buddhist religion, elusive and lacking in documentation as it might be, if we are to understand the fuller significance of the *Srin-mo* and her femininity.

5.

By the time the *Srin-mo* story is being told, the underdog religion is referred to as "Bon," and Buddhism portrays it as uncivilized, the perpetrator of such abominations as bloody sacrifice, and the cause of Tibetan ignorance and backwardness.[63] But this is not quite accurate. Actually, the term Bon is somewhat ambiguous, and certainly the general appellation as used now does not refer to the same set of religious beliefs and practices as the term did during the time of Srong btsan sgam po. In any case, Bon may well not be a truly indigenous Tibetan system; at least in large part it is itself foreign and may have suppressed yet an earlier strain of Tibetan religion.[64] If this is the case, then Buddhism, in characterizing Bon as barbaric and in need of suppression, may have been mimicking a pattern already established by Bon.

We have seen above that the Tibetans characterize their country as peopled by demonic spirits. It is known that much of early Tibetan religion was concerned with death. There abound rites dealing with the dead, leading them to other-worldly realms, and demarcating the difference between the realm of the living and that of the dead. Buddhist accounts attribute the act of "closing the door to the tombs of the dead" to the Bon religion.'[65] If this is so, and if our supine *Srin-mo* symbolizes what is truly indigenous in Tibetan religion, part of which is the fearful, (ir)repressible world of the demonic departed, then Buddhism was not the first to suppress her.

The *Grub mtha' shel gyi me long*, a late but well regarded account of the history of the religions of Tibet, singles out the suppression of the *Srin* and the *'Dre* as one of the primary activities of Bon, at least from the time of the quasi-mythical King Gri gum btsan po[66]. In the Tibetan epic, a *Srin-po*, this time male and nine-headed, is trounced and smashed by Gesar in order for the land of Gling to be created.[67] Even as early as the Tun-huang documents, the *Srin* is an evil force that has to be pressed down (*gnon*). In the text related to the sKyi Kingdom, and thought by F. W. Thomas to have been recited on the occasion of a scapegoat ceremony, the central event recounted is the holding down of the heads of various *Srin-pos*. Here, however, one of the principal suppressors is a female, "the Myang goddess who is master of the country."[68]

The suppression of the demonic and deathly may be related to a larger movement in Tibetan religious thinking. Abstracting traces from the complex and widely varying accounts of the Tibetan kings in the later mythologized literature, Erik Haarh detects a revolution in worldview that he associates with foreign invaders who usurped the Tibetan throne, at the time of the king gNya' khri btsan po and Gri (or Dri) gum btsan po. Part of this transformation has to do with a common Tibetan tripartite division of the world into underworld, surface, and sky, a division that Haarh wants to show was not clearly demarcated in the earlier period.[69] Instead, the early Tibetans focused most on the underground. Haarh theorizes that former kings were buried underground, or perhaps under water. Only after that tumultuous usurpment did it become important for the kings to be interred in tombs above ground. In accordance with this theory, the movement away from the underworld, and the introduction of the religious significance of the heavens (as one phrasing has it, "The Bonpos liked the sky"[70]) are exaggerated in the Tibetan myths about the early period. This tradition has the kings following gNya' khri btsan po ascending a "sky-rope" upon death. Again, the emphasis on the vertical.

Related to this line of speculation, as well as to the *Srin-mo* herself, is a revealing incident in the myth of Gri/Dri gum btsan po, portrayed as the king responsible for severing the sky-rope. Haarh identifies this incident as the occasion for the first above-ground burial of a Tibetan king. In an early version of the myth Dri gum's corpse is said to have been dropped first in the river.[71] In order to retrieve it, and place it in a tomb, his ministers were obliged to plead with the *Klu* spirits of the deep. We may note with interest that the *Klu* that relays the king's corpse back to the surface is a female; she is a messenger of a *Klu-srin*, and she herself is called *chu-srin*, "Srin of the water."[72] Is this mistress of the fate of the dead an aqueous sister of our land *Srin-mo*?

Forces of the deep, adversaries of the powers on high: cooperation with them is tenuous at best. Although the pieces don't quite fit together, we are approaching an understanding of how the *Srin* signifies what Buddhism was obliged to hold down. As for the femaleness of our *Srin-mo*, we have already seen that a number of factors concatenate. The land (what could be more indigenous?) as a Mother Earth; a tendency to characterize that which is uncontrolled and threatening as feminine; even some evidence that women held a powerful place in early Tibetan society. If that power was still in force at the time of the introduction of the Bon, and then the Buddhist religion—religions that are both propagated in the main by male figures—we can see why the haunted, superstitious Tibetan world might have been merged with that of a prominent femininity, to produce one trouble-making demoness.

6. ALL MERE PROPERTIES OR ATTRIBUTES MUST FOR MYTH BECOME BODIES[73]

In a postscript of sorts that appears in the *sBa-bzhed* chronicle, the fate of the supine demoness and her cohorts is bitterly denounced by King gLang dar ma, last of the Yar-lung monarchs. Notorious for his persecution of the Buddhists and his reversal of the policies of his predecessors,[74] he is here blaming the presence of the new religion for the famine, plague and crop loss afflicting his capitol. In an assembly in which he has summoned all of his subjects who are not ill, he demands,

> "What's the reason [for all of these disasters]? Do you know?" he asked.
>
> "We don't know," they said.
>
> "Well I know. There was a Gnod-sbyin devil called Kong cong[75] the Chinese. She brought the inauspicious god known as Śākyamuni and went to the top of Mt. Sumeru, disturbed the gods and destroyed them. Then she went to Urgyan and destroyed it. Then she went to Magada and destroyed it. Then she went to China and destroyed it. Then she went to Tibet, and being an expert at geomancy, she did geomancy. On the twenty-one spine bones of Mt. lCags-ka[76] that looks like a white lioness leaping into the sky, she put twenty-one *stūpas* as acupuncture pins (*me-rtsa*). She pressed down the head with a black *stūpa* with nine levels, and by making a temple on the top of the skull she pressed down the area of sTod. If she hadn't pressed that down, (we) would have conquered India. On the

> nose of Mt. dMar-po which looks like a tiger entering the nest of a mouse, she hammered in a wooden spike. If she hadn't done that, India would be under (our) control. She cut off Mt. Me-sna-gdong at Yar-lung, which looks like a rice sprout, at the neck. If she hadn't done that, Tibet wouldn't have a famine...[77]

Despite gLang dar ma's diatribe, he does not quarrel with the basic perception that the land of Tibet is constituted by beings, nor with the notion that such beings are affected by structures built on top of them. gLang dar ma is objecting only to the particular structures employed, the particular deities they house, and the places at which they are erected.

There is a very Tibetan proclivity to image features of the landscape, on both small and large scale, as animated. Ultimately, this tendency is to be related less to creation narratives—where the transformation of the primordial stuff into a civilized world space occurs in at least a quasi-temporal succession of events—as to a world view which must be seen as preeminently atemporal. Such a vision, similar to what Diana Eck has called a "sacramental natural ontology,"[78] is common in Asia and elsewhere, though a taxonomy of its many varieties cannot be laid out here. In Tibetan writing and thinking it is so pervasive that an entire volume could hardly explore it fully. The image ranges from one of a being who inhabits a given place (e.g. the numerous *Klus* who populate lakes and other parts of the underworld), to the place itself as constituting the spirit of a deity of some sort (as in the ubiquitous mountain cults[79]), to the perception of the actual contours of the land as being anthropomorphic or animal-like, by virtue of which that place is thought actually to be the being so outlined (as in our demoness story at hand). Such conceptions do not necessarily presuppose a narrative at all, but rather reflect some sort of projection of the elements of human perception onto the structure of the surrounding environment.

Once conceived, the *genius locii* is propitiated, appeased, protected, heeded, and valorized in myriad ways. It may also be violated, offended, and even wounded, as is the supine *Srin-mo*. The perpetrator of such offences can be anyone, and it is really a question of opinion or perspective as to whether a given action or construction is beneficial or harmful to the spirits of the land. Indeed, a Bon-po text also contains a self-congratulatory account of the disruption and suppression of the earth beings by buildings.[80] Be the spirit propitiated or suppressed, the point is that the analogical, animated, projective perception remains. It is a basic feature of what R. A. Stein calls the "nameless Tibetan religion." But it fully pervades organized Buddhism and Bon as well.

7.

In a perverse way, we might say that the supine, suppressed *Srin-mo* is actually kept alive and well by the very narrative of her domination. Certainly the fact that versions of her story are repeated in virtually every history of the early kings makes her difficult to forget. Supine *Srin-mo-s* are also to be found at the base of other monasteries, as related in their specific histories.[81] The striking image seems to be emblematic in Tibet of the very foundation of Buddhism.

One senses a certain pride in the description of the presence of the massive demoness. She reminds Tibetans of fierce and savage roots in their past. She also has much to say to the Tibetan female, notably more assertive than some of her Asian neighbors, with an independent identity, and a formidable one at that. So formidable that the masculine power structure of Tibetan myth had to go to great lengths to keep the female presence under control. And so we must beg to differ with Aris's characterization of our *Srin-mo*: she may have been ancient, and perhaps even virginal, but certainly she wasn't passively waiting to be subjugated. She was causing all sorts of havoc in the face of the incoming civilization, and required extensive Buddhist architecture, and narrative, to hold her down.

Srong btsan sgam po's erection of thirteen structures to suppress the *Srin-mo*, and later repetitions of the tale by other builders, constitute eloquent testimony to the continuing presence of the supine demoness. She may have been pinned, and rendered motionless, but she threatens to break loose at any relaxing of vigilance or deterioration of civilization. Indeed, the architectural erections insure her perdurance below; she provides no less than the organic unity of the land, the totality of the context in which civilization could thrive. In the final analysis, the very measures taken to subdue the *Srin-mo* have sustained her vitality in the Tibetan world.

3. *An Ecstatic Song by Lakṣmīṅkarā*

Translated by Miranda Shaw

Hail, Yamāntaka!

Lay your head on a block of butter and chop—
    break the blade of the axe!
The woodcutter laughs—
    a frog swallows an elephant!

It's amazing, Mekhalā—
    do not doubt!
If it confounds you, avadhūti-pa,
    drop concepts now!

My teacher didn't tell me,
    I didn't understand—
Flowers blossomed in the sky!

It's marvellous, Mekhalā—
    have no doubt!
If it confounds you, avadhūti-pa,
    drop your doubts!

A barren woman gives birth—
    a chair dances!
Because cotton is precious,
    the naked weep!

It's amazing, Mekhalā—
    do not doubt!
If you're incredulous, avadhūti-pa,
    drop your doubts!

Amazing—an elephant sits on a throne
    held up by two bees!
Incredible—the sightless lead!
    The mute speak!

It's amazing, Mekhalā—
    have no doubt!
If you're stunned, avadhūti-pa,
    drop your doubts!

Amazing—a mouse chases a cat!
An elephant flees from a drunken donkey!

It's marvellous, Mekhalā—
    do not doubt!
If you're stunned, avadhūti-pa,
    drop your doubts!

Amazing—a hungry monkey eats rocks!
Wonderful—the experience of the mind!
Who can express it?

Lakṣmīṅkarā (circa 8th century A.D.) was one of the accomplished practitioners, or "great adepts" (*mahāsiddhas*), whose careers mark the florescence of Tantric Buddhism in Pāla period India (8th-12th centuries A.D.). During its developmental phase in India, Tantric Buddhism was primarily a lay movement that evolved outside the boundaries of the powerful monasteries. This meant that women and men of all classes and occupations could pursue tantric practice while maintaining their familial responsibilities and jobs, although many did choose to leave their homes and wander throughout India, meditating in solitary retreats or congregating with other tantric yogis and yoginīs in remote caves, forests, and cremation grounds. This pattern brought to the palace of Lakṣmīṅkarā a tantric master who enabled the young princess to pursue intensive religious practice without becoming a nun. Lakṣmīṅkarā had been planning to marry and was betrothed to the king of Śri Lanka; but she decided not to marry when she discovered that her future husband was an impious and unrefined person. She chose instead to become a wandering yoginī, and practiced in solitary caves for many years, until she attained magical and yogic powers and finally *mahāmudrā-siddhi*, or enlightenment.

Lakṣmīṅkarā's influence as a tantric teacher and initiating guru was great. Her heroic resolve and religious intensity inspired her brother, King Indrabhūti, and her fiance, King Jalendra, to devote their lives to tantric practice. King Indrabhuti went on to become a great *siddha* and tantric author in his own right. King Jalendra wanted to apprentice himself to Lakṣmīṅkarā, but she assigned one of her disciples, a low-caste sweeper, to be his teacher. Some of her other famous disciples were Sahajayoginīcintā, Līlāvajra, Jālandharipa, and the *mahāsiddha* Virūpa.[1]

Because Lakṣmīṅkarā was a princess, she had access to an education and was thus literate, making it possible for her to record some of her practices and teachings in works that have been preserved in the Tibetan canon. Owing to her writings and from records of tantric transmission lineages, Lakṣmīṅkarā is known to have practiced the Six Yogas of Nāropa and meditation upon the female Buddha Vajrayoginī. Lakṣmīṅkarā's writings include a commentary on Indrabhūti's *Sahaja-siddhi*, a brief Vajrayoginī *sādhana* (practice manual), and a short work on Vajrayāna vows.[2] Her *Advayavajra*, which survives in Sanskrit as well as Tibetan, rejects formalistic practices and celebrates the nondual, spontaneous state of *sahaja* realization.[3] It also urges tantric practitioners not to disparage women, to worship women of all castes, and to realize that women embody nondual wisdom (*prajñā*).[4]

The standard literary genres of tantric literature, such as practice manuals and commentaries, record shared religious symbols and techniques rather than private religious experiences. However, *siddha-s* sometimes expressed their experiences in spontaneous, personal language in the form of songs, or *dohās*. Sometimes the songs were recorded by someone present when they were sung, and in this way a small sample of this delightful genre was preserved.[5] The colophon of Lakṣmīṅkarā's *dohā* says that it was "uttered" (Tib. *gsungs-pa*) by her and "transmitted" (Tib. *brgyud-pa*) by Mekhalā and Kankalā.[6] The sisters Mekhalā and Kankalā also were *mahāsiddhās*; though their acquaintance with Lakṣmīṅkarā is not recorded elsewhere. It was probably they who assigned the title, "Eliminating Mental Constructs," to the song.

Dohās were sung at moments of heightened awareness in an attempt to poetically express experiences that do not lend themselves to didactic expression. In this case, Lakṣmīṅkarā seeks to portray a state of mind that transcends dualistic thought-constructions. Such a song might induce in a receptive listener a glimpse of the nondual state. The nondual state reveals the magical indeterminateness of phenomena freed from limitation by dualistic concepts. This indeterminateness, or intrinsic identitylessness (*śūnyatā*), of phenomena occurs at several levels. One is the easily graspable fact that a phenomenon, such as water, is different in different contexts, becoming solid when frozen or evaporating when heated, and also different from different perspectives, so that it may appear as molten fire to a hungry ghost or as a crystal palace to a *nāga*. However, there is another level on which even these ordinary or predictable identities are abandoned, and *anything* becomes possible. At this level, water can laugh, flow upward, become fire, turn into gold, or undergo any transformation whatsoever. This is the level of special insight, or "aftermath wisdom" (*pṛṣṭhalabdhajñāna*), that follows exceptionally exalted states of consciousness and reveals the irreducible ordinariness of phenomena and at the same time their magical fluidity. This level of awareness frees perception from predetermined patterns and makes possible the utilization of illusions and miracles to liberate sentient beings.

Lakṣmīṅkarā's ecstatic song celebrates the magical quality of the nondual level of awareness. She bears testimony to the utter freedom of this level of experience by presenting startling, incongruous images, such as a frog swallowing an elephant and a chair dancing. Formal practice may have prepared the mind for such a state, but the final moment dawns spontaneously, like flowers blossoming in the sky. Lakṣmīṅkarā's listeners are urged to "drop concepts" and "drop doubts" in order to enter this state. She addresses "Meko" (presumably a nickname or form of address for Mekhalā), and also *avadhūti-pa*, a more general term for a practitioner of *gtummo* yoga or *rdzogs-rim* meditation, a process of concentrating energy in the *avadhūti* (central psychic channel of the body according to yogic physiology) that requires the cessation of dualistic thought. This song testifies to Lakṣmīṅkarā's realization and seeks, through vivid and paradoxical imagery, to convey the state of "crazy wisdom" to her listeners. Such states are best conveyed through poetry and song.

4. *Ḍākinī: Some Comments on Its Nature and Meaning*

Janice D. Willis

In the literature and tantric practice contexts of Tibetan Buddhism, the term *ḍākinī* (Skt.; Tib., *mkha' 'gro ma*) is fairly ubiquitous. Indeed, it occurs so often these days in Western translations of tantric texts, that one expects it will soon be appearing in *The American Heritage Dictionary* along with such other recently incorporated commonplaces as *satori*, *zen*, and *maṇḍala*. Still, apart from the quite literal definition of the term—i.e., as a feminine noun meaning "one who goes in the sky"—there remains little consensus about its meaning and, in my opinion, little precision in the various attempts to further delineate and characterize its nature and function.

Without doubt, *ḍākinī* represents one of the most important, potent, and dynamic images/ideas/symbols within all of Tantra. Yet, precisely owing to such dynamism and power, and to the all-encompassing nature of this symbol, it is almost impossible to pin it down or to limit it to a single definition. To do so is not the intention of the present essay. Instead, what I want to do briefly here is: firstly, to survey and review some of the diverse assessments of its meaning offered by scholars previously; and secondly, to suggest perhaps some new ways of thinking about it in a more holistic way.

Ḍākinī-s are said to be beings that are "tricky and playful."[1] The term is thus sometimes glossed by translations like "sky- dancer"[2] or "sky-enjoyer."[3] They are often described as "wrathful or semi-wrathful deities,"[4] though it is also recognized that they may have human (or other, animate or inanimate) form as well. In some contexts they are termed "demoniacal beings" and "witches."[5] One scholar seemed to like to call them "furies;"[6] others have referred to them as "sprites" and "fairies."[7] They have been called the "genii of meditation."[8] For tantric adepts, they are viewed as "messengers" or "prophetesses," "protectresses," and "inspirers." Additionally, they are at times regarded as *rig ma-s*, or "mystic consorts." And most inclusive of all, within Buddhist tantric contexts, *ḍākinī* is viewed as the supreme embodiment of the highest wisdom itself. Embracing such wisdom, one becomes Buddha.

I believe it is this latter sense of *ḍākinī*, that is, as the embodiment of the highest wisdom and as the symbolic concretization of the direct, unmediated, and non-conceptual experience of voidness (Skt., *śūnyatā*; Tib., *stoṅ pa ñid*), that makes the term so difficult to discuss. For in the ultimate, absolute, and final sense, "she" stands for ineffable reality itself. In a tantric universe replete with symbols, *ḍākinī*, one may say, is *the* symbol par excellence; and being preeminently, constitutively, and inherently *symbolic*, the *ḍākinī* always remains a symbol within the "Tibetan symbolic world."[9] As such, "she" serves always only to represent and suggest—even for the tantric adept—other and deeper, non-discursive experiential meanings. Inevitably, then, "she" remains elusive to academic or intellectual analyses.

All this notwithstanding, a number of scholars (western, Indian, and Tibetan) have offered various definitions, as well as symbolic and psychological interpretations, of the term. One extremely thoughtful analysis, by Nathan Katz, appeared in *The Tibet Journal* some ten years ago.[10] By way of review, I now turn to some of these.

1.
DEFINITIONS AND ETYMOLOGIES

In 1895, L. Austine Waddell's classic study of Tibetan Buddhism called *ḍākinī-s* "furies," further defined them as being synonymous with *yoginī-s*, and stated that both terms referred to "goddesses with magical powers."[11] In his estimation, it was because such "goddesses and she-devils were the bestowers of natural and supernatural powers and were especially malignant [that] they were especially worshipped."[12] S. C. Das's great *Dictionary*, which was finished shortly after that time, defined *mkha' 'gro ma* as "a class, mainly of female sprites, akin to our witches, but not necessarily ugly or deformed."[13] He went on to further delineate two types of such beings: "those still in the world and those that have passed out of the world"; and to include a group called the "goddesses of wisdom" (*ye śes kyi mkha' 'gro ma*) in the latter class.[14]

Some six decades later David Snellgrove would write, giving a much fuller description of *ḍākinī*, the following:

> Especially associated with Uḍḍiyāna is a class of feminine beings known as ḍākinī. There is frequent reference to them in the tantric texts, where they appear as the partners of the yogins, flocking around them when they visit the great places of pilgrimage. Their presence was essential to the performance of the psycho-sexual rites and their activities generally are so gruesome and obscene as to earn them quite properly the name witch. They enter Tibetan mythology in a rather more gentle aspect, and ceasing altogether to be beings of flesh and blood, they become the bestowers of mystic doctrines and bringers of divine offerings. They become the individual symbols of divine wisdom with which the meditator must mystically unite, and although iconographically they retain their fierce and gruesome forms, in such a context witch seems rather a harsh name for them. The Tibet-

> ans translated the name as sky-goer (mkha-'gro-ma), which Mr. Evans-Wentz regularly translates as fairy, but this scarcely does justice to their composite character.[15]

Snellgrove's description is certainly fuller, incorporating many of the ideas mentioned here earlier, while indicating still others.

A more recent study by Martin Kalff,[16] informs us further about the *ḍākinī's* pre-Buddhist origins, as well as "her" early iconographic representations. Kalff writes:

> The Ḍākinīs alluded to here [i.e., in the *Cakrasaṃvara Tantra*], female aspects of the enlightened Buddha, have to be differentiated from a lower type of Ḍākinī, a class of harmful female demons who feed on human meat. The relationship between the two types of Ḍākinī is suggested by the fact that the lower unenlightened type represents a remnant of a pre-Buddhist form which, with the ascendancy of Tantra, became integrated into Buddhism.[17]

Continuing his description of these "pre-Buddhist" demonic *ḍākinī-s*, Kalff notes:

> An example of the demonic type of Ḍākinī can be found in the *Laṅkāvatāra Sūtra*. In that text the one who eats meat is threatened with the following words:
>
> > From the womb of Ḍākinī he will be born in the meat-eaters' family and then into the womb of a Rākṣasī and a cat; he belongs to the lowest class of men.
>
> Here the Ḍākinī is mentioned in the same breath with a Rākṣasī, another type of meat-eating female demon who haunts the cemeteries. The Ḍākinīs, too, are at home in the cemeteries. They are very well described in a biography of Padmasambhava which includes his visit to eight cemeteries in eight different regions.[18]

Again, detailing his description of the "gruesome" iconographic depiction of these *ḍākinī*, Kalff quotes from Eva Dargyay's dissertation on the *Mātaraḥ* and *Ma mo*. Kalff's English translation of Dargyay's German reads as follows:

> And there is the uncountable host of Ḍākinīs. Some of them with loose hair ride on lions, in their hands they raise up the skull and the nine-pointed emblem of victory. Some of them are mounted on birds and they scream. In their hands they hold the lion's emblem of victory. Some of them have one body and ten faces. They eat intestines and hearts.[19]

In such wise are the "pre-Buddhist" *ḍākinī-s* described. Within Buddhism, however, a change occurs; and the *ḍākinī's* nature is softened and transformed. One may recall here, for example, that Padmasambhava's "journey to Tibet" is narrated almost solely in terms of his "tamings" and "subjugations" of various "demons" in route, the bulk of them female.[20] Following each such "taming," that demonic spirit being pledges to aid and support the new religion, i.e., Buddhism. Thence, the *ḍākinī* is viewed as a helper and an ally to the Buddhist cause. Now, as descriptions of "Buddhist" *ḍākinī-s*, we hear definitions like the following: "Dakinis, [or] female sky travelers, [are] the Tantric Goddesses who protect and serve the Tantric Doctrine. They are not invariably enlightened beings; there are many so-called Worldly Ḍākinīs. . .who are still bound in Saṃsāra."[21]

What then, one may ask, of the term's precise etymology? The Sanskrit term may have derived from a root meaning "to fly"[22]; but as the term is normally defined in the Sanskrit (at least, as evidenced by most of the *Purāṇic* literature), it refers to the "female attendants of Kali" who are said moreover to "feed on human flesh."[23] the Tibetan etymology certainly softens this portrayal of *ḍākinī*! In Tibetan, the equivalent for *ḍākinī* is composed of three syllables: *mkha'*, meaning "sky" or "space" (Skt., *ākāśa*); *'gro*, a verbal contraction meaning "to go;" and *ma*, a feminine particle marker. Hence, the compound term in Tibetan could justifiably be translated as "sky-goer" or "she who goes in the sky." Still, this does not fully explain the term.

I now cite three interpretations by Western scholars who attempt to offer further clarification of the Tibetan etymology. Herbert Guenther offers the following gloss: "The Tibetan explanation of the word for 'sky,' 'celestial space' is a term for 'no-thing-ness' (*stong-pa-nyid*) (Skt., *śūnyatā*) and 'to go' means 'to understand.' The Ḍākinī is therefore an understanding of no-thing-ness."[24] According to Anagarika Govinda,

> *mkha'* means "space" as well as "ether", the fifth element. . .in other words, that which makes *movement* possible. . .and makes form appear without being itself movement or appearance. . .*Hgro'* means "to go," "to move about". According to popular conception a *Khadoma* is therefore a heavenly being of female appearance (as indicated by the suffix *ma*), who partakes of the luminous nature of space or ether, in which she moves.[25]

Again, James Robinson, in a description which is perhaps too anthropomorphic (?), comments: "The Tibetans render dakini as *mkha' 'gro ma*, 'the sky-walking woman'. But the idea of 'sky' was interpreted as standing for 'emptiness', and 'walking' is equivalent to 'understanding', so that the dakini is 'the woman who understands emptiness', that is to say, the feminine embodiment of wisdom."[26]

SYMBOLIC AND PSYCHOLOGICAL INTERPRETATIONS

Individual terms function in contexts; and it is within such contexts that they take on life and meaning. (One is reminded of Wittgenstein's famed maxim that "the meaning of a word is its *use* in the language."[27]) Definitions and etymologies are useful only to a point. To begin to see what *ḍākinī means*, we need to see it in action, in context; that is to say, to see how it functions—as narrated in *siddha* biographies, as enacted in tantric ritual, and as depicted in tantric art.

Firstly, it is necessary—even if only briefly—to investigate its function in actual *texts*, i.e., what one scholar has called the role the *ḍākinī* plays in the "spiritual imagery" of Tibetan tantric texts.[28] As Katz rightly noted, among the chief sources for such an investigation are the biographies (Tib., *rnam thar*) of the *siddha-s* (tantric adepts who are famed for having attained Enlightenment in their lifetimes by using tantric means). Such texts are replete with mentions of the *ḍākinī*; and the stories they narrate are told and re-told throughout the Tibetan world of practice. Undoubtedly, one of the most famous stories is that which narrates the episode of Nāropa's encounter with the grand dame of all *ḍākinī-s*, the great Vajrayoginī. As wonderfully translated by Guenther,[29] this story goes as follows:

> Once when 'Jigs-med grags-pa (Abhayakīrti [=Nāropa]), with his back to the sun, was studying the books on grammar, epistemology, spiritual precepts, and logic, a terrifying shadow fell on them. Looking around he saw behind him an old woman with thirty-seven ugly features: her eyes were red and deep-hollowed; her hair was fox-coloured and dishevelled; her forehead large and protruding; her face had many wrinkles and was shrivelled up; her ears were long and lumpy; her nose was twisted and inflamed; she had a yellow beard streaked with white; her mouth was distorted and gaping; her teeth were turned in and decayed; her tongue made chewing noises and licked her lips; she whistled when she yawned; she was weeping and tears ran down her cheeks; she was shivering and panting for breath; her complexion was darkish blue; her skin rough and thick; her body bent and askew; her neck curved; she was hump-backed; and, being lame, she supported herself on a stick. She said to Nāropa: "What are you looking into?"
>
> "I study the books on grammar, epistemology,

> spiritual precepts, and logic," he replied.
> "Do you understand them?"
> "Yes."
> "Do you understand the words or the sense?"
> "The words."
>
> The old woman was delighted, rocked with laughter, and began to dance waving her stick in the air. Thinking that she might feel still happier, Nāropa added: "I also understand the sense." But then the woman began to weep and tremble and she threw her stick down.
>
> "How is it that you were happy when I said that I understood the words, but became miserable when I added that I also understood the sense?"
>
> "I felt happy because you, a great scholar, did not lie and frankly admitted that you only understood the words. But I felt sad when you told a lie by stating that you understood the sense, which you do not."
>
> "Who, then, understands the sense?"
>
> "My brother."
>
> "Introduce me to him wherever he may be."
>
> "Go yourself, pay your respects to him, and beg him that you may come to grasp the sense."
>
> With these words the old woman disappeared like a rainbow in the sky.

(It has been my experience that whenever I have asked a Lama to explain to me the nature and meaning of *ḍākinī*, he has answered, firstly, by narrating this particular story!)

Guenther, applying Karl Jasper's term, has called *ḍākinī-s* "ciphers of transcendence."[30] In the "Introduction" to his translation of Nāropa's *rnam thar* he posits his own interpretation of the above passage:

> The vision which induced Nāropa to resign from his post and to abandon worldly honours, was that of an old and ugly woman who mercilessly revealed to him

> his psychological state. . . . All that he had neglected and failed to develop was symbolically revealed to him as the vision of an old and ugly woman. She is old because all that the female symbol stands for, emotionally and passionately moving, is older than the cold rationality of the intellect which itself could not be if it were not supported by feelings and moods which it usually misconceives and misjudges. And she is ugly, because that which she stands for has not been allowed to become alive or only in an undeveloped and distorted manner. Lastly, she is a deity because all that is not incorporated in the conscious mental makeup of the individual and appears other-than and more-than himself is, traditionally, spoken of as the divine. Thus he himself is the old, ugly, and divine woman, who in the religious symbolism of the Tantras is the deity rDo-rje phag-mo (Vajravārāhī) and who in a psychological setting acts as 'messenger' (*pho-ña*).[31]

The *siddha* biographies give us numerous other examples of the "play" of the *ḍākinī*. Another example of the *ḍākinī* as shock-therapist is provided by the *rnam thar* of Abhayākaragupta. As translated by B. N. Datta, the pertinent passage reads as follows:

> Once, as he was sitting in the court of [a] temple cloister, there appeared a young maiden who dragged on a piece of beef near to him which was dripping in blood, shoved it to the acarya and said: "I am a Candāla [out-caste] maiden, but eat what is slaughtered for you." But he answered: "I am a Bhiksu of purer order. How shall I eat meat which is extraordinarily offered to me?" But she sank back and disappeared in the court below. That was again Vajrayoginī who gave him the Siddhi, but he did not take it.[32]

Like Nāropa (in later sections of his *rnam thar*), Abhayākaragupta here missed his chance to attain special power and insight even though the *ḍākinī* offered him the opportunity (read: "chance," "moment," or "space") in which to do so. The *ḍākinī-s* burst upon the scene (here, consciousness) at any moment, to test, to shock, to "stop the [habitual] world"[33] of the future *siddha*. Thus they may be said to function as "tricksters."

As "messengers" they are often also "triggers," "instigators," or "inspirers." Again, as Katz has noted, "the influence of the *mkha' 'gro ma* is virtually [a] universal [motif] in *rnam thar* to mark the 'turning-point' stage."[34] "Her" appearance catches the future *siddha's* attention, and creates a space in which old, habitual, patterns are either mildly called into question, or shattered completely. Indeed, it is because "she" ushers in insight which is totally new, and because the experience of insight seems to *burst* in upon the intellectually barren and stagnant mind, that the *ḍākinī* is described as "playful" and "capricious." Of course, "her" very abruptness also explains why "she" is also so often described as "horrific" and "terrifying."

As "trickster," the *ḍākinī tests* the tantric adept in numerous ways, usually revealing his or her own mental rigidness and neurosis. Commenting upon this "trickster" quality of the *ḍākinī*, Trungpa Rinpoche has said:

> The playful maiden is all-present. She loves you. She hates you. Without her your life would be continual boredom. But she continually plays tricks on you. When you want to get rid of her she clings. To get rid of her is to get rid of your own body—she is that close. In Tantric literature she is referred to as the dakini principle. The dakini is playful. She gambles with your life.[35]

The *ḍākinī* is not always, however, a terrifying messenger. Sometimes in various *rnam thar* we see "her" as trusted companion and prophetess. In the *rnam thar* of rGyal-ba dbEn-sapa,[36] for example, the following passage is found:

During that time [rGyal-ba dbEn-sa-pa] occupied himself performing penances and behaving in such a way as to have [the experience of] Bliss-Voidness arise [continuously] in his consciousness. Then by the Wisdom-Ḍākinī he was advised thusly: "Tomorrow you will meet a paṇḍita who is the reincarnation of the great siddha dPal-'bras-rdo-rje. To that one you should impart all the detailed practice instructions without holding back."

While the above example contains implicit reference to the *ḍākinī* principle in "her" iconographic form as the great Vajrayoginī, other *rnam thar* refer to this principle in other forms, whether deific, human, or formless. For example, from the *rnam thar* of Saṅs-rgyas-ye-śes we learn that he determined not to remain in Lha-sa (but to return to his Mahāmudrā guru—i.e., dbEn-sa-pa—in gTsaṅ) on account of 1) a mysterious illness, and 2) a dream in which a "young girl" admonished him to do so. The pertinent passage reads:

> . . .when Saṅs-rgyas-ye-śes had developed the illness in his legs while in Lha-sa, he had strongly determined at that time to return to gTsaṅ as soon as his illness left him. Moreover, it had also happened that one night in a dream, a young girl had said to him, "Now you have accomplished your aims (here). Let's go back go gTsaṅ!"

Just prior to this passage and interestingly, offered as an "explanation" of it, one finds another passage in the *rnam thar* which alludes to the *ḍākinī* by way of showing its influential presence and workings in the spiritual life of dbEn-sa-pa, himself. This passage states:

> Now, in the meantime, it had occurred that an inner voice spoke to. . .dbEn-sa-pa, saying, "It is good that my Rab-'byams-pa [i.e., Saṅs-rgyas-ye-śes] has not wandered too far away. I must ask [the great goddess] dPal-ldan Lha-mo to bring my brilliant one back to

> me, since his remaining [in Lha-sa] could be harmful [to him]."

The *coda* which connects and encapsulates these two passages is intriguing, both for its picturing of the inner dynamics of spiritual clairvoyance and telekinesis, and for the tender and loving concern it illustrates in connection with the guru-disciple relationship. The text says, "This explains why. . . [Saṅs-rgyas-ye-śes decided to return to gTsaṅ]" and, finally, "Those events occurred owing to dbEn-sa-pa's feelings of concern [for his heart-disciple]." Moreover, it may be noted that in these two passages, Saṅs-rgyas-ye-śes' illness, dbEn-sa-pa's "inner voice," the grand protective deity dPal-ldan Lha-mo, and the "young girl" in the dream are *all* manifestations of the *ḍākinī*.

In the above examples, a certain pattern can be clearly discerned. Namely, the appearance of the *ḍākinī* in each case marks a particular and unique *communicative moment* for the tantric adept. In terms of specific functions, during such moments, or "spaces," "she" prophesies to, advises, or carries out the wishes of, the advanced adept. For the *siddha*-to-be, she provides protection. Manifesting in multifarious forms, "she" serves as the spur, inspiration, and helpful companion for successfully accomplishing the arduous path of tantric practice.

In order to perform such functions, the *ḍākinī* does not always manifest as a phantom of dreams, nor as the divine apparition of a deity. Nor does "she" necessarily take human form. In one account "she" appears as a stone statue.[37] In the *rnam thar* of the *siddha*, Kukkuripa, the *ḍākinī* is his dog![38]

Still, if we judge from the evidence of the *siddha* biographies, we note that quite often the *ḍākinī* does appear in human, female form; and that in this form, "she" is often the sexual partner or "mystic consort" (Tib., *rig ma*)[39] of the *siddha*. Such human *ḍākinī-s* are integrally and intimately connected with the sexual symbolism of tantric ritual and practice and, by extension, to the notion that for certain advanced tantric practices, the aid of an actual flesh and blood partner is useful and/or required.[40] According to Katz's count, "fully fifty-six of the eighty-four [Indian *mahāsiddha-s*] are depicted in the company of a woman."[41] Citing examples, Katz notes:

> The attainment of mahāmudrāsiddhi by Vaidyāpāda is dependent upon his taking up residence with a Candāla [outcaste woman]. Anaṅgavajra is instructed by his guru, Padmavajra: "Put yourself in touch with the swine-keeping woman by keeping swine and then step by step you will be a Vajrasattva." . . . .We hear of Dha-ri-ka-pa, a king, becoming the servant of a harlot. Pu-ta-lo-ki in the same verse ". . .won the harlot and perfection."[42]

And, of course, owing to recent English translations, we are all quite familiar now with such illustrious human *ḍākinī-s* as Ni-gu-ma[43] ("wife" of the *siddha*, Nāropa, who developed and taught her own system of the famed "six yoga-s"), Ye-śes-mtsho-rgyal[44] (chief Tibetan consort of Padmasambhava), bDag-med-ma[45] (Marpa's accomplished wife), and Ma-gcig-lab-sgron-ma[46] (Pha Dam-pa Saṅs-rgyas' chief consort, and fashioner of the advanced meditative system of *gCod*). These examples remind us that the Tantras were, and remain, effective for producing enlightened beings regardless of sex. They should also remind us that these were no ordinary women practitioners! They were all tantric masters in their own right, who left society's constraints to follow the treacherous path of tantric practice. (It should be stressed, moreover, that within the contexts of certain advanced tantric practices, the processes of sexual intercourse may be performed either between human partners or conducted solely as an internal and imagined series of yogic actions. In the case of human practitioners, the sexual act is not performed by "ordinary beings," but rather by "deities"; by beings who have each put aside his or her ordinary mind-body complex and assumed the arcane body and the subtle awareness of a particular deity.)

Summarizing the major functions of the *ḍākinī* in the tantric *siddha* biographical tradition—what one might call a summary of the *ḍākinī* as a central *leit motif*—Katz has enumerated the following:

> 1) inspiring and directing the siddha; 2) directly or indirectly initiating the siddha; 3) [serving as] the patron of the siddha. . . 4) the source of power of the siddha; 5) guardians of the *gter-ma*; and 6) biographers of the siddha.''[47]

He goes on to reiterate that, ''The *mkha' 'gro ma* may appear in visions, dreams, meditations and as actual women. They are also revered as preceptors of particular yogic practices [i.e., *gCod*; *gTum-mo*] and may be demoniacal as well as beneficent. . .Their role in the lives of the siddha is tremendous. . .''[48]

It remains now only necessary to mention how the *ḍākinī* functions within the contexts and symbolism of tantric ritual and practice, itself. According to the symbolism of tantric, or Vajrayāna, Buddhism, Enlightenment (*bodhi*) is represented as the perfect ''sexual union'' (Skt., *yuganaddha*; Tib., *zuṅ 'jug*) of ultimate wisdom and compassionate activity. In Mahāyāna Buddhism generally, these two are referred to as *prajñā* (Skt.; Tib., *śes rab*) and *upāya* (Skt.; Tib., *thabs*), respectively. *Prajñā* is represented as being female; and *upāya*, as being male. (Of course, the perfection of sexual union, simultaneous orgasm, is a familiar and direct symbol for the loss of ''self''—what might be called a readily understandable description of *śūnyatā*. During such orgasm, both partners experience the ''transcendental emotion'' called in the Tantras, *samarasa* or ''one taste.'' Here, neither partner is distinct. It is impossible to distinguish where one ends and the other begins. This experience of ''wholeness'' and ''sameness'' is accompanied by intensely blissful feeling.)

In terms of tantric symbolism, these two are iconographically represented as two deities, usually semi-wrathful in form, who are embracing in sexual union. The pair of deities are said to be in the aspect of *yab-yum* (Tib., literally, "Father-Mother"). Comprising this most reverred pair are the great Wisdom-*ḍākinī* (Tib., *Ye-śes-mkha'-'gro-ma*) who is usually in her form as the Goddess Vajrayoginī or Vajravārāhī,[49] and "her" consort (whether Cakrasaṃvara, Guhyasamāja, Hevajra or whatever chief "male" deity of the given ritual cycle). Their blissful union symbolizes complete Enlightenment, the direct, blissful experience of ultimate Voidness.

Since our discussion focuses on the *ḍākinī*, it is fitting here to describe "her" *deific* form. To do so, I refer to one of "her" chief iconographic forms, that is, as the great *yi dam*, the Goddess Vajrayoginī:

> Her body is a vibrant blood-red color. Apart from the bone ornaments that are draped around her waist and a necklace of skulls around her neck, she is completely naked. She holds aloft in her raised left hand a *kapāla* [Skt.; a skull cup, here, filled with amṛta]; and her right hand wields a hooked knife [Skt., *kartari*]. Resting upon her left shoulder is the trident staff, or *khatvāṅga* [that represents her consort, the Heruka, Cakrasaṃvara]. The top of the staff is decorated with three skulls. Standing with bent left leg and outstretched right leg upon two corpses, her entire figure is encircled in flames.[50]

In such wise is "she" envisioned and contemplated upon by the practicing adept.

2.
OVERVIEW AND CONCLUDING REMARKS

In the above materials, in addition to briefly reviewing how some scholars have defined and interpreted the phenomenon of *ḍākinī*, I have tried to indicate a sampling of the multiplicity of forms and guises in which the symbol, or principle, of *ḍākinī* manifests. To be sure, such a multiplicity of forms, together with the fact of "her" special ambiguity—i.e., that "she" is at once the witch, the trickster, and wisdom incarnate—combine to make "her" a most *elusive* phenomenon. Yet, in spite of such divergent images "her" nature, it seems to me, is *allusive* as well. Viewing the *ḍākinī* in a number of different textual and ritual practice contexts allows us perhaps to develop some appreciation of its multivalent character. Here, then, I wish to offer some general comments regarding "her" nature and meaning.

To begin, it allows us to note that "she" is *not* "female." Though the *ḍākinī* assuredly most often appears in female form (whether as a female deity, or a female human being), this is but one of the *myriad* of ways Absolute Insight chooses to make manifest its facticity. Modern-day women practitioners who pride themselves on being "already half way there" owing solely to their sex, need only be reminded of two pristine teachings on Voidness:

In the *Diamond-cutter (of doubts) sutra*,[51] the Buddha said:

> Those who by my form did see me,
> And those who followed me by my voice,
> Wrong the efforts they engaged in,
> Me those people will not see.
>
> From the Dharma (alone) should one see the Buddhas,
> From the Dharmakaya comes their guidance.
> Yet Dharma's true nature cannot be discerned,
> And no one can be conscious of it as an object.[52]

And, in the *Vimalakīrti-nirdeśa-sūtra*, the goddess who lives in Vimalakīrti's house (herself a *ḍākinī*!) has this dialogue with Śāriputra (who represents the conservatism of early Buddhism wherein distinctions based on sex still held sway):

> *Śāriputra*: Goddess, what prevents you from transforming yourself out of your female state?
> *Goddess*: Although I have sought my 'female state' for these twelve years, I have not yet found it. Reverend Śāriputra, if a magician were to incarnate a woman by

> magic, would you ask her, 'What prevents you from transforming yourself out of your female state?'
> *Śāriputra*: No! Such a woman would not really exist, so what would there be to transform?
> *Goddess*: Just so, Reverend Śāriputra, all things do not really exist.[53]

(Of course, modern-day men practitioners who think this lets them off the hook from respecting their female counterparts might reflect upon the last of the "Fourteen Root Vows of Vajrayāna," which makes it clear that it is a serious downfall "to disparage women, who are of the nature of wisdom"!)[54]

The *ḍākinī* is, however, a *feminine* principle. The term used to refer to the phenomenon is a feminine noun; and within the tantric symbolism employed to represent supreme Enlightenment, the *ḍākinī* most assuredly takes feminine form. Of course, one of the most interesting questions in this regard is, "why is *that* the case?"[55] An attempted answer would require at least a book; but I would like to suggest that apart from such ancient characterizations, constructs, and divisions based on sex and/or gender differences—as for example, "male=intellect, female=intuition;" "male=activity, female=passivity and receptivity;" and the like—the main idea being articulated here is that the *ḍākinī* is the *necessary complement*[56] to render us (whether male or female) whole beings. To put it another way, "she" is what is lacking, the lacking of which prevents our complete Enlightenment.

Given that we un-Enlightened beings normally exist in rather narrowly limited "spaces," it is not surprising that the appearance in our lives of the *ḍākinī's* vastness ("she" is *all* that we lack!) might be, at least initially, overwhelming, horrific and terrifying. Some of the portrayals of the *ḍākinī* as "gruesome, demonic, flesh-eating ghouls" no doubt spring from this perspective. And with the most stubborn and most self-righteous, "she" is least gentle!

Making contact with the *ḍākinī*, then, is sometimes terrifying and always dangerous; but doing so offers the chance for dramatic and highly-prized fruit. The biographies of the *siddha-s* show that these brave ones actually seek "her" out. To do so, they are usually shown making perilous journeys and visiting cemeteries and charnel grounds. The "logic" of such imagery operates on several levels at once. The "outer" journey, of course, is more accurately, an "inner" or "spiritual" one; and because in order to fully make contact with "her," the adept's own ordinary psycho-physical being must "die," the cemetery is a most appropriate symbolic place for such an encounter. Even in non-tantric Buddhism, the utter destruction of the "false idea of a 'self'" must be accomplished prior to (or concomitant with) the attainment of the insight which cognizes Voidness (*śūnyatā*) directly. Having finally won access to the *ḍākinī*, the tantric adept is thereafter graced by "her" to receive new powers and insight and, ultimately, full Enlightenment itself.

From the absolute point of view, then, the *ḍākinī* is highest wisdom, itself. That is, "she" is the direct, unmediated, nonconceptual understanding of Voidness (*śūnyatā*). "She" is, as her chief iconographic representation suggests, the "naked" experience of Voidness, in itself—limitless, uncontained, effusive, and entirely blissful. How could such an experience be adequately described in words?

In the tantric world of ritual and meditative practice, the older Buddhist trilogy of *Buddha*, *Dharma*, and *Saṅgha* is replaced by the triad of *bLa ma*, *yi dam*, and *mkha' 'gro ma* (i.e., *ḍākinī*). But in practice, each of the three includes both of the other members of the triad; so that one regards one guru as the *yi dam* and as the *ḍākinī* (since both are *embodiments* of the highest wisdom). Likewise, the *ḍākinī* is both *bLa ma* and *Yi dam*. In highest tantra practice contexts, one is continually reminded that about this, one should not be confused. The *ḍākinī* is all the "Three Roots" in one.

Within tantric contexts (and Mahāyāna contexts, generally), we speak of the *trikāya*, or so-called "Three Bodies of the Buddha." Since "she" embodies the highest wisdom, the *ḍākinī* is all three of these bodies. "She" is the formless "Body of

Truth," the *Dharmakāya*. In "her" communicative role, bringing inspiration and insight to advanced practitioners, "she" is the magnificent and eloquent "Enjoyment Body," the *yi dam*, or *Saṃbhogakāya*. And in "her" infinite manifestations which serve to communciate with us ordinary beings and to trigger havoc in our habitual *saṃsāric* patterns of thought, "she" sports in countless configurations of the "Emanation Body," the *Nirmāṇakāya*. The *ḍākinī* is thus, in her vastness, the embodiment of the entirety of *trikāya*.

Also within the world of tantric *practice*, another triad is commonly posited, namely that which delineates the "outer, inner, and secret" (Tib., *phyi*, *naṅ*, and *gsaṅ ba*) levels of experience. (These three may be seen as reflecting the *trikāya*, in reverse order.) According to this manner of speaking, we may say that the *outer ḍākinī* is those varied forms in which the *ḍākinī* appears, whether human or deific, benign or wrathful, beneficient or malevolent; the *inner ḍākinī* manifests when the advanced meditator successfully transforms him or herself into the great *ḍākinī* (usually Vajrayoginī, herself); and the *secret ḍākinī* is the formless power, energy, and pure bliss of Voidness.[57]

In this last aspect, the *ḍākinī* is synonymous with another extremely important concept in the Tantras, namely, *Mahāmudrā*, the "Great Gesture" or "Great Symbol"; for "she" appears when the highest intellectual grasp of Voidness is transcended. There since beginningless time, "she" is the ultimate, unchanging, basis and reality of being. At the end of the arduous path of practice of highest yoga tantra, "she" reveals "herself," naked before us. And regardless of whether we are "male" or "female" beings, if we wish to become Enlightened beings, we must embrace, and be embraced by, "her."

5. *Moving Towards A Sociology Of Tibet*

Barbara Nimri Aziz

A sociology of Tibet can begin with a study of its women and its men. As yet, however, there is no sociology of Tibet. Regrettable as this is, as difficult as this makes cross-cultural comparisons between Tibetans and others, studies of this culture do not permit us to see it as a whole social system. To change this, there is no better place to start than with the analysis of Tibetan women. Coming so late, at least there is the advantage of having at our disposal today the findings of two decades of Women's Studies with the sophisticated social analysis they now afford, leaping over the decades of sociological work outdated because it failed to take into consideration the role and myths of women's positions. Beginning with basic social markers, we can consider them as gender markers—terms of address, preferential behavior, division of labor—and move through them to economic roles, access to power, expectations and achievements, and of course, symbolic meanings and associations derived from ritual and myth.

My readers will know from this introduction that in addressing women in Tibetan society, I am not talking about a confined sphere of activity but a universal issue. Eleanor Leacock pointed out in 1981 that "To handle women's participation in a given society with brief remarks about food production and child care has until recently met the requirements of adequate ethnography.[1] Before that, historian Gerda Lerner pointed out that our task was not simply compensatory history, or the chronicling of "women worthies"; it was to be an investigation of our patterns of thought and a questioning of our basic suppositions. With those warnings, women's studies expanded to raise basic questions about all social behavior and cultural beliefs. For anthropologists as well as historians and scholars in religion this meant a re-evaluation of all we had accumulated in half a century of painstaking, conscientious research.

In the past two decades Women's Studies in all fields of inquiry has moved ahead with massive strides; first it refined research methods, then it broadened the definition of social data and finally it identified the theoretical implications of that new knowledge. Meanwhile, our work in Tibetan society and culture stagnates, unable to contribute to cross-cultural comparative research and incapable of clarifying basic issues for Tibetology.

In separate papers, Anne Klein[2] and I[3] have already pointed to discrepancies in existing images of women in Tibet. In her study, Klein concludes:

> . . . the presence of an egalitarian principle cannot automatically translate into an egalitarian society. The lack of widespread social egalitarianism suggests the extent to which the major principle of Buddhism can be lost and it raises questions about socioeconomic, psychological and other factors adversely affecting women."[4]

(This is after Klein examines the case of the famous Ayu Khandro where she considers social conditions rather than superhuman achievements.) Her approach heeds Janice Willis' warning that stories of miraculous women cannot be the basis for grasping social realities.[5] Klein's concern is to test the social impact of those divine female models prominent in Tibetan

Buddhism. At the same time she questions how far Buddhism (or any other religious ideology) bears on social reality. She confronts basic inequalities she finds are experienced by Tibetan women. To Klein, furthermore, the Tibetan case is another example of religion's failure to translate its core principles into social reality.

I find myself in agreement with Klein's critical view of religion and with her interpretation of the social condition of Tibetan women. However, there is another prevailing view, namely that women in this culture enjoy extraordinary liberties and a status not so different from men. This was the claim of an experienced and highly capable researcher, Beatrice Miller, in her 1980 paper "Views of Women's Roles in Buddhist Tibet."[6] Her review results from inductive reasoning based on the premise that Tibetan Buddhism itself is an egalitarian ideology.

The appeal of egalitarian Buddhist philosophies on the one hand, and of feminist perspectives on the other, now confronts us, calling for an early clarification. It creates a legitimate, indeed a pressing demand for solid, reliable sociological data about this culture, data of a degree we have never had, neither for men nor for women. This thus becomes a point from which to launch a sociology of Tibet.

Below I outline a case study of women at work based on recent observations in Lhasa city. First however, let me review some possible subjects for gender analysis in this culture, Tibetan practices whose tradition we need not speculate over. Moreover, we need not skirt issues by assembling fragments from aristocrats' careers, or by arguing that a comprehensive picture of traditional gender values is now impossible to convey because conditions have changed so radically in communist dominated Tibet on the one hand, or in the diaspora on the other. In and outside Tibet, it is possible to observe women in different situations today, to talk with them, to ask why they prefer one thing and not another. They will say what are their expectations, the obstacles they confront, and what goes on in spheres neither divine nor monastic, communities where most people live and where culture is generated and maintained. From what we learn, we may be able to suggest what social factors impinge on and inspire an ordinary life cycle of a woman or a man.

The practices and attitudes I review below, I myself saw among both refugees in the diaspora and Tibetan people living in Tibet today. They embody values which are widespread and they reflect the persistence of significant gender differences in this culture. They also suggest what being a woman or a man probably means in societies such as Ladakhi and Lepcha (in India) and Sherpa, Tamang and Limbu (in Nepal) which are fundamentally Tibetan, so strong has the influence from the northern civilization been.

Let us begin with *language*. In Tibet now and among Tibetans living in exile, the common term for woman is *skye-dman*. It is not a new word; and it is not slang or a localized term. The word appears in early texts as well as modern documents. More common than *bud-med*, a colloquial term, *skye-dman* doubles for wife—another's partner as well as one's own. So one regularly hears men refer to their wife as *nga'i skye-dman*.

Now the meaning. Literally this word translates "born low." This rather alarming signification is not buried in the distant past nor in the unconscious. Anyone using or hearing it can tell you precisely what it means. They will also agree that no equivalent term exists for "man" or for "husband". Males are addressed as *khyo-ga, skye-pa* (also signifying adult or manhood) or *bu*. *Khyo* carries a sense of heroic, upstanding; *bu* is boy; it is also used honorifically, e.g. Bu Tsering, for sons of a high status family; this also applies to their daughters, addressed as *bu-mo*.

As for pronouns, here again strong gender differences exist. "She" is variously spoken as *mo, mo-rang*, or *khyo* for the majority of women and by the suffix *yum* in cases of divine or aristocratic status. *Mo* is the most commonly used. Men adopt *mo* in reference to wives and daughters just as they do to strangers. Furthermore, *mo* regularly applies to any destitute woman and to the female animal as the pronoun "it."

Mo is suffixed to nouns to create the feminine form, e.g. bitch (*khyi-mo*), mare (*rta-mo*), ewe (*lug-mo*), sow (*phag-mo*), she-devil (*bdud-mo*), and so forth. (Carrying a sense of disrespect, *mo* never applies to one's mother, or to a noblewoman or a goddess.) The parallel suffix for males, *pho* or *po*, is not similarly used as the pronoun "he." "He" is most often expressed as *kho* or *kho-rang*: these two terms apply to women only occasionally, namely when one consciously intends to denote respect. They never apply in a general way to animals i.e., "it" or "they." As far as I am aware, destitute men or male servants or minors do not receive a special pronoun. The diminutive "he" would be simply *kho*, which I have already pointed out is considered a respectful way of referring to women.

If language has any social significance at all, these terms should alert us to a serious gender difference in Tibetan culture, one that places the woman in an unequivocally inferior position. It provides undeniable evidence that women in this society are less exalted than Western observers have been led to believe. The situation is even more seriously imbalanced for women clerics in Tibet. However, their treatment is not within the scope of this paper. Since other scholars are, I believe, addressing the sociology of Tibetan nuns, specialized papers about them should soon be forthcoming. I limit this paper to a discussion of laywomen, although some remarks may apply to nuns who, as children, were subject to the same forces. I also try to exclude references to the conspicuous but small aristocratic sector of this society, where economic factors can safely be assumed to significantly alter the norm.

As spare as the data is, we have some facts from which to begin and to move forward, guided by the impressive assemblage of material resulting from women's studies of gender status and symbols from across the world. Those studies and this review are not concerned with how hard women work, how they care for their young, or how sexually accessible women are. They look at how a civilization is defined, how periods of history are marked, how status is expressed, who holds and wields authority, how access is gained to different realms of knowledge and power, what being female means, and finally, what people themselves consider auspicious, or evil, impotent, defiled or weak, in reference to men and women.

Taking *skye-dman* as our starting point. . .this word carries a conscious social status that Tibetans everywhere recognize as low. Yes, they say, a woman is not as capable as a man, she cannot enter into new areas of development; her place is in the house; she lacks a man's intellectual capacity; she is unable to initiate new things; and finally, she cannot become a Bodhisattva until she is reborn as a man.

From the instant a person is born these attitudes start working. In Tibet, being "born low" is institutionalized from the outset of a girl's life. First, no parent is pleased over the birth of a girl as they are by the arrival of a son. This is not a suppressed value; it is openly stated. And a man without a male heir is believed, and said to be, most unfortunate.

In a recent paper I refer to the discreet private rituals which explicitly illustrate the higher value of sons.[7] Beginning with his birth, his sexuality is considered a precious thing which is auspicious and which must be protected. Charms are used to prevent his being kidnapped by jealous witches, or transforming into a girl.

Infant girls are not killed here as they are in some parts of the world; nor are they usually sold into slavery by their parents. Yet, they clearly fare less well than their brothers. For example, the life of an illegitimate girl child is usually quite wretched, strikingly so compared with a boy who will have opportunities to share his father's social and economic status.[8] Even in their rightful families, a sister must begin laboring at an earlier age; and she is subject to harsher treatment than her brothers. In the home, she is the first one up in the morning, stoking the fire, fetching fuel and water, and so forth. She assumes his domestic duties when a brother is sent to school; while she herself is still a child, she becomes like a junior mother caring for other siblings; and the child sent to help an ailing or destitute relative is invariably a teenage girl. A boy sent as a servant to a monk-uncle has a far better chance of becoming educated and promoted to higher monastic ranks than has a girl who attends a nun relative. And so on. These practices are recognized as being widespread throughout the world today. Now we can confidently include Tibetan society as one which similarly assigns women to greater hardships while limiting her opportunities.

These references I base not on fragments from traditional Tibet but on today's practices and on the comments I observed among Tibetans in India and Nepal during a long association with Tibetans, and more recently, in a brief visit to Tibet. They are traditions which continue in widely differing cultural contexts today, a sign (perhaps) of their deep rooted character. (They may also have been strengthened by outside factors, circumstances I discuss in my paper, "Women in Tibetan Society and Tibetology.")

This kind of behavioral evidence and whatever else we know about social realities can be evaluated against egalitarian claims of Buddhism, as Klein is doing. But they should also be considered in relation to how women appear in popular secular and religious literary sources. Literature, religious and otherwise, presents models, ideologically re-inforcing these discriminatory attitudes. Especially outside Tibet, people use Buddhist texts, proverbs, myths and songs to sanction their choices and support their claims. From Milarepa to Aku-tamba, and across an infinite range of songs and stories we can see that heroic individuals are men, that women are secondary figures often applying their influence surreptitiously or through chicanery. Reading this literature, we see women's chief concerns are material gain; their merits are beauty and suffering. We know they are the hell-travelers (*'das-log-ma*), but are they Shambhala visitors?[9] We need not be reminded that Tibetan women are characterized also as the most compassionate and patient members of society. And the "feminine mystique" also seems well established in this culture with constant invocations of woman's compromising, tempering role, of her faculty for forgiving and her capacity for seducing, of her work as instigator and as ally.

Should we not wonder why Ma-gcig Lab-sgron is considered by Tibetans, including those who champion her, as a liberated prostitute? Is this a particular case, we ask, or is there a frequent association of this kind? From the literature we know that women are a chief obstacle in men's path to liberation; numerous tales illustrate that. But what according to those stories are the normative impediments and challenges that face women? What are the recurring themes in regards to women? What in them are presented as the chief elements of conflict, power, ill-fortune or success for women?

To begin this investigation of Tibetan culture, Diana Paul's collection and analysis of common Buddhist stories is exemplary, a model for the necessary parallel research we are calling for.[10] It was begun in Indian Studies long ago, largely through the contributions of O'Flaherty.[11] Her symbolic analyses of Hindu myths and early Vedic poetry reveal powerful gender meanings. This kind of work has generated a number of similarly insightful analyses, among them studies of nearby Himalayan cultures such as Lynn Bennett's work among Nepal's Chetri-Brahman women.[12] She and others[13] try to take the symbolic analysis further, illustrating how those religious symbols reflect conditions of society.

With the abundance of Tibetan literary materials carrying accounts of both common experiences and fantastic ones, we would do well to reread them with a more critical eye to their general implications for women in the society. Reginald Ray has attempted this in his brief review of the life of the *mahāsiddha*, Lakṣmīnkarā.[14] Even so, he admits that the (lady) *siddha* histories he examines are "problematic" because of their fantastic nature. Ray was less concerned with the social realities of Tibetan women than with Vajrayāna Buddhism's potential for both men and women. Yet we commend his efforts in opening the literature to other scholars.

The symbolic reading of Tibetan texts was finally begun by Robert Paul, in his recent book entitled *The Tibetan Symbolic World*.[15] The widely read life of Yogi Milarepa, The Tibetan Gesar-king of Ling epic, and four drama stories are among the well-known Tibetan materials which anthropologist Paul reviews and analyzes with a view to identifying accompanying symbols associated in this culture with political and sacred authority. (That key symbol he describes as an Oedipal one, itself concerned directly with the problem of the succession generations.) To start, it does not matter that this anthropologist's interests are not in gender dynamics. It is the approach to literature that can be instructive for us. Morever, whether or not one accepts Paul's Freudian approaches to Tibetan religion, we can, by watching this author decipher the code, begin to see other ways of looking at such stories besides the one which advocates meditation as a solution to all social ills. Paul systematically breaks down each story, forcing us to look at the components, to consider analogies and secondary meanings in repeated arrangements of symbolic images or events. Without going so far as to suggest any Western psychoanalytic order to things Tibetan (I am neither an adherent of the universal applicability of Freudian thought, nor a symbolic anthropologist myself), I propose that, noting Paul's approach, we might begin to see patterns in the way gender differences are expressed in Tibet, patterns which actually affect adherents' expectations of themselves—girls or boys, women or men. Doing this, we may begin to explain the workings of what we repeatedly claim, namely that in this society, religion is the basis of all cultural experience.

One of the most productive sources of women's experience worldwide is the life history, either autobiographical or third person accounts. In the former, we have only two from Tibet,[16] one of which is by the famous aristocrat. Biographies of Tibetan women currently available are of one sort, namely the fabulous accomplishments of outstanding divine women. This area of Tibetan religious history, long overdue and so shamefully overlooked, was opened by Tsultrim Allione with her balanced and valuable collection of the lives of six Tibetan lady saints.[17] Those stories furnish glimpses of some of the obstacles women confronted en route to enlightenment. These moving portraits and Allione's summary of the feminine in Tibetan Buddhism open an important chapter in the study of Buddhism. Yet, it must be recognized that they refer to a special realm; as Ray and Willis note, these are rare examples and cannot be a basis for a sociology of women. What we require to balance and complement these are accounts of more regular lives, those of nuns or laywomen, which portray both childhood and adulthood. And, whether we work with people now living in Tibet or with women outside its borders who now follow a very different lifestyle, their biographies promise to be a valuable resource.

Tibetan women, prompted to write their own life accounts, can make a lasting contribution here; in some cases we scholars and friends may ourselves undertake to be their scribes. Looking at our own culture, any number of lives from our Western histories, uncovered or newly written in recent years, have had immense impact on women's studies, just as autobiographies of Black Americans have opened new frontiers on Black culture and history in the U.S.A. Among the most notable women's writings in our culture are de Beauvoir's *The Second Sex* and *Memoires of a Dutiful Daughter*, Thurman's *Izak Dineson*, Nin's *Diaries*, and Hong Kingston's *Woman Warrior*. Alexandra David-Neel's two volumes of letters (*Journal de Voyage*) as well as her travelogues on Tibet have had wide impact. The list of influential books on women is now enormous and growing at a rapid rate.

Anthropological contributions to women's biography in general are not as many as they could be; yet we might mention *Women of the Shadows, Daughter of Han, Let Me Speak, Baba of Karo,* and *Nisa*.

Oddly, no scholar today has attempted to write a firsthand biography of a Tibetan woman—as enchanted as we are with the people of Tibet, as urgent as we feel about their culture. (Turnbull's fine co-authored autobiography of T. Norbu, *Tibet is My Country*, or the history of the Karmapa lineage, even Trungpa's *Born in Tibet* are a different genre. In any case, each of these is the story of a Tibetan man, and more especially—a Lama!)

Biography is a potentially rich field for us to pursue. We need not be concerned if the woman is not a celebrity, and for our purposes it really does not matter if she lives in Tibet or in exile. Whatever we write is bound to be of value, and if we do not delay, the stories will contain a great deal on the times and life in pre-communist Tibet. Whatever the focus of those stories or however they are styled, they are bound to be laden with the kind of data which when gathered form various sources can indicate general conditions. They thereby serve sociology as well as literature and history.

A CASE STUDY FROM LHASA, 1986

The second part of this article is a case study not from literature or biography. It is a sociological portrait of a small community of workers. It draws on my recent brief stay in Lhasa and describes gender relations in a modern new hotel serving foreigners. Let us call the place "Palaceview".

What follows is not meant to be a thorough anthropological portrait; nor can it be taken as typical. It is more of an example of how a sociological study can begin, and what can be read about women from some very basic facts. Even though the hotel is newly established and has direct contact with outsiders, this does not preclude it as a valid source of sociological data.

"Palaceview" is one of three new hotels built in old Lhasa to accommodate the recent sudden increase of young tourists, foreign backpackers traveling through Tibet on low budgets. When I stayed there in the summer of 1986 it was eighteen months old and still expanding.

In winter, "Palaceview" is not very busy. It operates on half staff then, with only a third of its rooms open, housing visiting Qinghai and Kham businessmen and other visitors calling themselves pilgrims. Summer months by contrast are overflowing; all 40 rooms are filled with foreign tourists. They occupy all 270 beds and require a full staff of 31 on hand seven days a week and working long hours. Facilities are extensive;

besides the sleeping quarters there are additional income-producing facilities: hot showers, bike rental, restaurant, dry goods retail store, tea room. All staff are Tibetans who also serve as the co-op officers. The co-op is autonomous but is responsible to a government tourist office and the health department whose officers are both Han and Tibetan.

The hotel's staff positions break down as follows: bike-repair and rental (two workers); shopclerks and stockperson (three); accountants (four); kitchen staff (four); reception (four); showers (three); tearoom (one); security (two); room attendants (seven); chief administrator (one).

Most staff members are relatively young; the oldest, the manager, is hardly 50. All have basic education in Tibetan and a few can read and speak Chinese. Once a fortnight internal management meetings occur which all 31 workers must attend. Men and women seem to be equally vocal at such meetings which are chaired by the manager.

This egalitarian structure seems to apply in the daily operation with respect to male and female employees. More than half the staff (19 out of the 31) are young women aged 25-40. Like the men, they wear slacks or denim jeans, shirts or blouses, and tailored jackets. These are in no way militaristic and they are not uniform; they are attractive, youthful garments now fashionable among most city workers. The women also sport stylish wide-brim hats, earrings, and heeled shoes. Three of the four reception staff and all seven room attendants are women and more than half of them are married.

These ten workers have the closest contact with hotel guests. Such exchange is intense with the usual degree of exuberance, flirtation and gentleness that characterizes Tibetans. Every evening two of the young women, assigned to night duty, stroll through the hotel corridors; frequently they sit talking with guests in the rooms. Because of this degree of personal contact with guests these women are acquiring a smattering of English, Japanese and Cantonese (many guests are from Hong Kong). Everyone, workers and visitors, takes pleasure in the popular and folk songs (Tibetan) they sing during their work.

Their presence provides a convivial atmosphere which everyone clearly enjoys.

This contrasts with the male staff who generally maintain their distance from visitors. The two lads renting bikes are more sober and less conversant; the cook, a man, also speaks far less to customers than do the women who work beside him. Only the interpreter in the reception office, a young man from India, is more forthcoming when on the job; but he is never as gregarious as his women co-workers.

In summary the women staff of "Palaceview" are in positions which facilitate the most contact with hotel guests. They provide direct services of hot water, room service, food, registration. In this capacity they are also hostesses, maintaining an ongoing convivial dialogue with hotel guests which is both refreshing and proper, never overstepping the bounds of discretion, but appearing to be informal and spontaneous—in contrast with anyone we encounter in Indian or Chinese hotels. It is strikingly different from one's impression of Han, especially those one meets in Lhasa. Everyone visiting Lhasa whom I meet remarks on the aloofness and inattentiveness of the Han workers who are in contact with them. They appear to decline personal contact with us. Women as well as men seem to maintain a distance, and there is always a regrettable formality, brusqueness and disinterest during contact. Furthermore, we are unable to see young Han men and women engaging in public repartee like the Tibetans. (This may not characterize Han attitudes in China proper; indeed I have noted much more intimate behavior of Han to visitors.)

These Tibetan women fulfill our earlier image of being approachable and fun. Not unexpectedly, they receive frequent invitations for dinner and disco dancing from male guests. (They invariably decline, as far as I know). Even if their convivial nature is administratively encouraged, their behavior derives from a certain temperament, a facility with outsiders, and a license with men. That is not confined to guests; one sees the women flirting and bantering with male staff at the hotel. Their manner echoes what we experience among Tibetans in

India or Nepal. It appears they enjoy parity with men and are prominent in public life.

However, when we look at the structure of the hotel administration, this egalitarian image is not carried through at more basic levels. The manager and security staff are men; the chief cook is a young man and so are the bike attendants and the chief shopkeeper, and three of the four accountants. Although male staff are fewer in number at "Palaceview," they hold all the senior positions and they are the chief decision makers. The manager of the restaurant, the security officer in charge of rooms and reception are men; so is the chief accountant.

Thus all 19 women here are supervised by men, and no woman holds an administrative post in the entire hotel complex. This means of course that women are not as directly involved in decision making. But there are other implications. While excluded from positions of power, women nevertheless carry the heaviest burden of labor. I have already mentioned their key role with the public, occupying the front line where there is greatest contact with guests, where they must exert ingenuity and initiative.

Less apparent is the physical burden they bear. Only the women must rotate on night duty, leaving their homes and families for a week once every two months. Furthermore, they are the lowest paid. With a monthly salary of 110 Yuan ($30) per month they are lower paid than the cook, the security guard, the shopkeeper, the accountants. When bonuses are distributed among workers from the co-op profits, these women earn a share, but it invariably is less than the share allocated to managers. Since no tipping is permitted or expected in the service roles, there is no supplemental income from that source.

Finally and most significantly, the 13 women who are room and shower attendants and assistant cooks have the least pleasant jobs. They clean the latrines daily; they wash the used dishes and scrub down the kitchen; they chop meat and vegetables; they clean the shower-rooms and stoke the woodburning boiler; they launder sheets and towels and empty the rooms of litter and stale food; it is also they who must shovel the week's accumulated offal from a common bin into a dump truck. On two occasions during my stay, when corpses of dogs lay rigid in the courtyard of the hotel, it was these women who were instructed to dispose of them. Their burden is compounded by the general lack of facilities. Remember that plumbing in Lhasa is minimal and hot water and drainboards are not available for dishwashing, so these jobs are more disagreeable than they would be in the worst of our hotels. Add to this the common illnesses of high-altitude and food poisoning that frequently turn a hotel room into a sickroom. With no nursing care available, it is the maids who clean up the mess.

Keep in mind that this work proceeds in a congenial atmosphere. As I described, a joking, sometimes intimate relationship is maintained between male and female employees here. Furthermore, there is no class division or caste stigma attached to anyone here. These women do not belong to a different class nor do they come from a region of Tibet that might mark them as a different ethnic group. Furthermore, I cannot portray the men as lazy and arrogant. They are industrious and friendly, fully occupied and attentive in their supervisory jobs. Occasionally, such as before the health inspector's visit, they will lend a hand in sweeping the yard and clearing garbage. But this does not alter the consensus that the dirty work is women's.

When I brought the issue up with two "Palaceview" employees who I felt I knew well enough to share my observations with, neither seemed startled and neither disagreed. It was they who went on to generalize: "That's the way it is among Tibetans; cleaning toilets and interiors is women's work. They have to do it." "Could the hotel not hire men to do some of it?" I suggested. I was told firmly that no man would do these jobs, that they would refuse. The same person added that women are accustomed to the dirty jobs.

I had not detected resentment or opposition by the women, but the inequity seemed so gross that I was puzzled about the women's feelings on this matter. One supervisor admitted that indeed, the women were displeased; they had, he said, complained about an unfair share of the messier jobs. Furthermore, I was told, they had asked for promotion into some of the management positions, and they were upset when this was denied. The women were also disturbed that the one man in reception was selected for training in English and relieved from work half of each day for that reason while the women were passed over. When this fellow eventually abandoned his language training, again the women were not offered the chance and when I left the hotel, another young man from the bike shop was in line for English training. It is an assignment that will surely lead to advanced power and increased salary.

It would be unfair and not much use for me to make generalizations based on this single case; I myself consider this account far from complete. There are doubtless a number of factors, internal as well as imposed from outside which are still unknown about the way the hotel personnel are managed. We do not know the policy of the tourist office which oversees the hotel administration; we are uncertain to what degree Chinese and socialist values are involved here. Moreover, the hotel is itself an unusual institution in Tibet and it may be run rather differently from other offices or factories.

Nevertheless certain issues are all too familiar: the sociable, gregarious and forthright manner of young women towards strangers; the repartee between men and women employees; the attention of women in inside jobs and that of men to outside work; and men's refusal to take on certain "dirty" jobs. True, one is unlikley to find women as outgoing as this elsewhere in Asia, women with almost no prior contact with strangers, who move with such confidence and engage so discreetly. It is possible that they enjoy this license as long as they provide cheap labor. But the situation is not that simple and that conclusion is not yet substantiated or justified. Furthermore, we cannot rush to the conclusion that attitudes we find favorable are founded on Tibetan tradition whereas those we disdain are imposed by Chinese socialist policies. Among all these ramifications, I find two conditions of special significance:

One is the refusal by Tibetan men to clean latrines and sweep rooms. This could be an outcome of specific localized conditions, but I doubt that. It is more likely defined by general Tibetan Buddhist beliefs about women's polluted status—an essential issue about which we know almost nothing. However, where information from related communities is available, we cannot deny clear associations of women's work and condition with sin. A new reference is Fisher's recently published study of the Magar trading people near Dolpo, Nepal. In his discussion of the division of labor, the author notes quite unequivocally that only women here do polluting work—work involving direct contact with excrement (including fertilizer from fields), human or animal.[18]

The second noteworthy condition is those women's request for additional power and a greater role in management. They do not hide their disaffection.

To assemble a clearer picture of their situation, starting with what we see here, we can ask a number of related questions. We need to know about the organization of the co-op: does it have bylaws which impose limits on the work and management role of women employees? Does it demand investment by its workers which women for some reason cannot afford? Are women not permitted to hold shares, and if so, what is the basis for such exclusion? On the other side, we want to know what are the career goals of the women? What do they see as benefits for the burden they bear in the cleaning load?—there may be some unseen advantages to their acquiescence. Do they have another career goal and are only biding time in this job? Do they consider the personal contact they enjoy with guests compensatory for their unpleasant duties? Is that contact a privilege or yet another humiliation? Interviews with the women about their roles will doubtless point up a number of factors at work. (I intend to follow up this report with such discussions as well as gather information about the co-op charter and its management rules.) When we feel we have a full picture of women in this community, then we need to move to a parallel organizational situation—perhaps a carpet factory co-op in Kathmandu, or a co-op store in Musoorie. After gathering like data, we may then ask the same questions and compare the characters of several.

Even in the strikingly untraditional contexts of wage labor at the "Palaceview" Hotel or at a Thamel (Kathmandu) retail store, we might expect a woman's family values and networks to bear on what working conditions she accepts. Thus, we seek out information next about her siblings and her parents: their education and work, their level of prosperity, and so forth. Women's work is recognized as an arena which bears directly on her general status and self-esteem as well as others' attitudes towards her. This is why the subject of women's work is the focus of a number of breakthrough studies in economics today. Leacock and Safa's collection, *Women's Work*[19] investigates this area of society and shows irrefutably how the sexual division of labor worldwide, is a fundamental social division whereby men dominate over women. This separation is promoted and reinforced either through capitalist economics or through patriarchal ideology; it is often both.

We all recognize the value of women's labor. No Tibetan—no one—will deny the essential role a woman plays in the economic success of her household. We do not question this. What we ask is why she nevertheless lacks a stronger voice, and why her prestige is so low compared with any man's. We need to note if and how a woman attempts to convert her valued role as laborer into one of power. Failure to try or to succeed may be due to the effect of cultural models at work suppressing her ambitions, subordinating them to her husband's, channeling her into religion, or teaching her how later rewards accrue if she shows patience and endurance now. Conclusive evidence will certainly emerge both from the subtle suggestions of cultural practice and from overt pedagogy imbedded in Tibetan religious ritual and scripture and in other forms of literature.

We shall doubtless find women portrayed in working roles in the literature. We might also identify work tools such as spindles and milkpails, looms, and horse-bridles. These items, so essential to a Tibetan's livelihood, emerge at some level in stories, in rituals, in myths, in songs. Recently two authors, anthropologists Kaplanian[20] and March,[21] noting the appearance of certain key cultural instruments in myth and song, began their probe of gender values there.

Starting with a review of Ladakhi myths of human origin, Kaplanian notes the central imagery of male and female spindles. (In Ladakh and Tibet, both sexes employ spindles but they are designed and used in different ways and with different fabrics). Kaplanian, examining the character of those spindles to determine their meaning in culture, suggests these tools symbolize the opposition between masculine and feminine. Not only that; he illustrates how they help to (culturally) define the assignment of males to the outside, and females to the house. He goes on to show how these symbols play in a variety of contexts to associate women with land, or earth.[22] With Tibetan and Ladakhi culture sharing so much, we might profitably compare his findings against parallel Tibetan myths.

The same value can be drawn from March's study among Nepal's Tamang people, a highland Buddhist people who probably originated in Tibet. She examines the imagery of cloth-weaving and its relation to writing among the Tamang, beginning thus:

> For the Tamang, both weaving and writing are not only technical skills but dense symbols of gender. They are gender symbols not only because they tell the Tamang about the separate roles of sexes, but because they are about what transpires between the sexes as each defines the other. Two opposing conceptions of the world emerge as Tamang men and women view one another; gender symbolizes both the opposition and the reflexivity of these world views.[23]

(The same hypothesis can be read for male and female symbols from Kaplanian's argument.)

Neither of these examples derive from pure Tibetan cultures although Ladakhi and Tamang people are closely related to Tibetans. Because of that, it is reasonable to compare theirs with Tibetan symbols of weaving and writing, and the spindles. Can we apply March's proposition to Tibetan weaving? And if not, why? Is it because values in Tibet are substantially different, or might it be due to our complete ignorance of how weaving and related concepts work in this culture? In either case, or both, it seems to me it is time to find out. This means approaching Tibetan society sociologically.

How far such symbolic analyses will support or otherwise test what I have described of the workers in "Palaceview" at this point depends on how honestly we are prepared to pursue the sociology of Tibet. Only when we make an attempt in this direction will cross-cultural studies become relevant to our area and will we benefit from the abundance of knowledge already uncovered by research in gender relations across human history.

Just as studies of gender today are studies of an entire social system, so such a pioneer study of women in Tibet could serve to open up a sociology of all its people. I make my representations as a beginning, not as an end. We can hope that if women in this society are as dynamic and as public as is believed, in beginning a study of Tibet with this focus, we will have already placed ourselves on a central axis of the society.

6. *Tibetan* Ani-s: *The Nun's Life in Tibet*

Janice D. Willis

1.

> I am a woman—I have little power to resist danger.
> Because of my inferior birth, everyone attacks me.
> If I go as a beggar, dogs attack me.
> If I have wealth and food, bandits attack me.
> If I do a great deal, the locals attack me.
> If I do nothing, gossips attack me.
> If anything goes wrong, they all attack me.
> Whatever I do, I have no chance for happiness.
> Because I am a woman, it is hard to follow the Dharma.
> It is hard even to stay alive![1]

These words were spoken by Ye-śes-mtsho-rgyal, one of the two chief tantric consorts of "Guru Rinpoche," that is, Padmasambhava, the Indian *siddha* (or, tantric master) credited with having "established" Buddhism in Tibet.[2] The quote is taken from mTsho-rgyal's *rnam thar* or "complete liberation life story" (in many respects an equivalent of hagiographies or "sacred biographies" in the West).[3]

Now though she may sound in the passage above a bit *burdened* by the female form, in an episode just prior to this one, her tantric accomplishments have been publicly praised by the Guru in words like the following:

> Wonderful yoginī, practitioner of the secret teachings!
> The basis for realizing enlightenment is a human body.
> Male or female—there is no great difference.
> But if she develops the mind bent on enlightenment,
> the woman's body is better.
> From beginningless time,
> you have accumulated merit and wisdom,
> Now your good qualities are flawless—
> what an excellent woman you have become, a true Bodhisattma!
> Are you not the embodiment of bliss?
> Now that you have achieved what you wanted for yourself,
> strive for the benefit of others.[4]

Recently a number of studies have begun to appear which address the issue of women as religious practitioners in both Western and non-Western cultures.[5] Women's place within Buddhism has proven to be a fertile area of investigation and several treatments have appeared which discuss the various portrayals of women in Buddhist literature.[6] However, analyses limited solely to the literary sphere invariably neglect a good deal of what constituted, or constitutes, the day-to-day world of religious practice.[7]

The topic of women and Tibetan Buddhism and of women's place within Tibetan Buddhist religious life has received considerably less attention and remains to be explored in full. While there are—in the vast corpus of Tibetan scriptural literature—examples of perhaps a dozen or so women who have risen to eminence within the tradition (and about whom *rnam thar* have thus been composed)[8] the religious life of the far larger group of unsung ordinary women practitioners has received little or no attention at all. And yet, it is precisely these "unspoken worlds" of the uncelebrated Tibetan women practitioners that offer the most potential for revealing religious life as actually lived and practiced in Tibet. It is hoped that the present article, which focuses on the lives of five Tibetan Buddhist nuns, will help to illumine that religious life a bit better.

In Tibet, prior to 1959, there existed a number of different types of women *chos-pa*[9], or religious practitioners. There were women *lha-kha-s* and *dpa'-mo-s* (i.e., "spirit-mediums");[10] there were female religious bards called *ma-ṇi-pa-s*; and—representing what may be viewed as the two poles of Buddhist practice—there were the tantric adepts (like Ye-śes-mtsho-rgyal) and the *ani-s*, or Buddhist nuns. To be sure, the type of women lauded in the sacred annals are the accomplished tantric practitioners: women like Ni-gu-ma, "wife" of the Indian *siddha*, Nāropa, who developed and taught her own system of the famed "six yogas." There is bDag-med-ma, Marpa's accomplished wife; and Ma-gcig-lab-sgron-ma, Pha Dam-pa Saṅs-rgyas' chief consort and fashioner of the advanced meditative *gCod* rite.[11]

Though there are fewer sacred biographies of women tantric adepts than of their male counterparts, such biographies do nevertheless exist and they evidence that the Tantras were, and remain, effective for producing enlightened beings regardless of sex. But these women are the rare and fabulous examples. They are all tantric masters, having left society's constraints to follow the treacherous path conducive only for a chosen few. And, all these women are *mudrā-s*, or "consorts" (to male tantric practitioners). Some are referred to simply as *yoginī-s*; others are called human *ḍākinī-s*, i.e., incarnations of the feminine principle of insight and wisdom itself. They are not your ordinary everyday Tibetan women practitioners.

On the other end of the spectrum there are the Tibetan Buddhist nuns, women who have quietly, and often with great difficulties, continued to practice in accordance with the monastic rules laid down at Buddhism's very inception in India, c. sixth century B.C. About this type of enrobed female practitioner the texts do not speak and very little information is presently available. No indigenous Tibetan literature, of whatever historical period, focuses upon them. Moreover only the most scant attention has been paid to them in the very recent past. Yet the *ani* tradition has managed to survive.[12]

In what follows I wish to look more closely at the *ani* tradition in Tibet. And so, leaving aside the fabulous women of the *rnam thar*, my aim here is to focus upon a set of life histories of five Tibetan *ani-s* of the twentieth century. Two of these *ani* were well known figures in Tibet. The other three, including Ani Dol-kar (sGrol-dkar) whom I personally interviewed in Nepal in 1980, are simple practitioners to whom little or no attention has been paid previously. I believe that the lives of these *ani-s* can shed a great deal of light on how Buddhism functioned in the lives of Tibetans (both men and women), and on how it was actually practiced by them. Again, the issue of women serves as an entrée into the larger question of the social world of religious practice.

2.

Before proceeding to describe the case histories themselves, some general—though often overlooked or misconstrued—features of the Tibetan religious landscape need to be noted. In the past, the failure of many Western explorers and scholars to accurately depict and weigh certain geographic, demographic, and linguistic features of Tibet has resulted in a quite distorted picture of Tibetan religious life.

Because Tibet (or, *Kha-ba-can*, the "Abode of Snows") is situated virtually at the top of the world and is fortified on three sides by many of the highest mountains on earth, the country itself until very recently was famed for its very remoteness and inaccessibility. Those few travellers and explorers who managed to reach Lhasa, Tibet's capital city (the name means "Dwelling Place of the Gods")—men like Heinrich Harrer, Marco Pallis and even Lowell Thomas, Jr.—told of its magic and mysteries in grandiose and idealized fashion. Tibet was depicted as a type of "shangri-la," as a country where the sheer vastness and stark beauty of nature itself caused heightened awareness; where peace reigned eternally, where the Buddhist religion permeated all facets of life at all times; where celibate monks and nuns were prized above all other citizens and where such clerics—by the thousands—chose to live a life apart in cloistered enclaves continually engaged in religious endeavors. Such descriptions are a bit too idyllic and much too idealized. They present a static, capital-centered view of Tibetan life. A truer picture of Tibetan Buddhism, Tibetan monasticism and Tibetan religious life would show it to be much more dynamic, bustling, diverse, and fluid.

Most Western accounts seem unaware of Tibet's actual demography, of its distinction between town and village hamlet, and of the quite striking fact that only 1/75th of Tibet's pre-1959 population was "urban." No accurate census was ever taken of Tibet's three chief regions (*chol-kha-gsum*) prior to 1959 but estimates put the overall population figure at between 4.5 million and 6 million. Basing his analysis on the 6 million figure, Shakabpa[13] has suggested that of this number 48 per cent of ethnic Tibetans were nomads, 32 per cent were traders and agriculturalists, and 20 per cent were clerics. His estimates are that 18 per cent of these latter were monks and 2 per cent were nuns. (This would mean that in Tibet some 1,080,000 men were monks as compared to 120,000 nuns—or roughly 9 monks to every nun.)[14]

As Shakabpa also notes, there were only four large cities, or towns in all of Tibet:[15] *Lhasa*, the capital, with a population which ranged normally between 35,000 and 40,000 (but expanded to as many as 70,000 or 80,000 during the Tibetan New Year, when clerics and pilgrims converged for the Great Prayer Festival [*Mon-lam*]); *Shigatse*, with a population ranging between 13,000 and 20,000; *Chamdo* with a population of between 9,000 and 12,000; and *Gyantse* (for which Shakabpa gives no figures). By Tibetan standards these were bustling cities to be sure and they were also the sites of some of the largest and most celebrated monastic institutions. But their combined population figures would only count some 57,000 to 72,000 (say 80,000 counting Gyantse) ethnic Tibetans to be urban city-dwellers—or roughly 1/75th of all Tibetans. The rest of the population lived (and carried on their religious lives) in much smaller towns and village hamlets, scattered throughout the vast one and a half million square miles of the country.

In another important respect, Western capital-centered views of Tibet have resulted in distortion of Tibetan religious life. Namely, such accounts have misconstrued the nature and degree of celibacy among the various Buddhist sects. There are four major schools or sects of Tibetan Buddhism—the rNying-ma-pa, the Sa-skya-pa, the bKa'-brgyud-pa, and the dGe-lugs-pa. In modern times (actually, since the seventeenth century), the dGe-lugs-pa has enjoyed political dominance, the Dalai Lamas all being trained in this "reformed" tradition. Of the four schools, only the dGe-lugs-pa enjoins strict celibacy, and then only upon its religious elite. While "Lamas" (or venerated teachers) in the other three "non-reformed" sects *may* be celibate, a life of strict chastity is nowhere enjoined upon all religious practitioners; and the ideals of the non-celibate tantric *yogin* are always upheld. Early Western travellers, going to Lhasa, saw the three massive dGe-lugs monastic complexes built nearby: 'Bras-spungs, Se-ra, and dGa'-ldan. With monk populations of 9,000, 7,000, and 3,000-5,000, respectively, these *gdan-sa-gsum* ("three great sees") gave the impression no doubt that Tibet was a land of celibate monks and monasteries. But just as Lhasa was not representative of all of Tibet, this capital-centered view told only part of the story.

Lastly, even the language used by Western scholars to describe the central institution around which much of Tibetan religious life revolves has suffered distortion. Thus the word *dgon-pa*, usually translated as "monastery," in Tibetan means "any solitary place where meditative practice can be carried on."[16] The term is used both with reference to an isolated retreat spot or to any settlement where men/women have gathered together to practice the religious life. Among the "unreformed" sects, there are countless so-called *ser-khyim dgon-pa*, that is, religious communities comprised of married clerics. Such *ser-khyim* members are tantric practitioners and ritual experts, who, while performing priestly duties and being affiliated with a *dgon-pa*, still live as householders. Such an arrangement probably would appear odd to outsiders who have other notions about what a "monastery" or "convent" means.

Even when primarily celibate establishments, most *dgon-pa* were not usually designated or distinguished as being strictly either monasteries or nunneries, though one sometimes comes across the designation *ani-dgon-pa* (i.e,. "nunnery").[17] The more common arrangement seems to have been a joint venture wherein groups of nuns were appendaged to monasteries or inhabited a given area of a monastic compound.

Because most *dgon-pa* in Tibet were small rural establishments, close ties existed between village and *dgon-pa*. Speaking of this relationship, Snellgrove has remarked:

> Apart from a number of very large monasteries. . .and some medium sized monasteries with five hundred monks or so, other Tibetan monasteries were comparatively small with fifty to two hundred monks, and often far less. These small communities possessed little or no land and depended for their existence mainly on the families whose members were actually monks. Thus most monasteries developed in close relationship with nearby villages, providing for the religious, educational and in large part the cultural needs of the community. Monks and layfolk lived in such close association, joining in so many activities together, that it completely falsifies the real nature of Tibetan society if one sets monks in opposition to layfolk. . .[18]

For the majority of Tibetans, these close ties and close distances accounted for fairly continuous movement back and forth between village and *dgon-pa*. A palpable connection existed between the secular and the religious life. Indeed for most Tibetan *chos-pa* (i.e., *religieux*), to separate them completely would have been not only impractical, but a falsification of the actual workings of their religious practice.

Holding all the various types of religious communities together was the Lama, or teacher. He or she was the center and cement of the community. Yet the styles of teachers were as diverse and individualistic as the teachers themselves. There is an old Tibetan saying which goes: "Every ten *li* (Chinese, "three miles"), heaven is different. Each district has its way of speaking; each Lama his way of teaching." The Lama set the tone for a particular religious community and area; and his or her distinctiveness was mirrored by the members of the community. What Barbara Aziz has noted for the inhabitants of D'ing-ri could easily be applied more broadly. She writes:

> Paralleling the range of life styles exhibited by their *la-ma*, D'ing-ri novices make a choice as to how they will proceed. The religious life is one that symbolizes free choice and so there is no one to dictate a religious style to the new initiate. Each therefore begins life as a *ch'o-pa* according to individual circumstances. An *a-ni* may remain with her family for many years (if she gets on well with her brother's *na-ma*); or immediately after her ordination she may go on a major pilgrimage to parts beyond D'ing-ri where she had never been before. She may opt to live with a kinswoman in a *gon-pa* or she may become an itinerant and avoid any permanent home for years. Such a range of possibilities is also open to the new *dr'a'-pa* [i.e., a male *chos-pa*]. And after following any one for a time, it is not unusual for the devotee to shift to another style.[19]

Indeed a great deal of religious freedom seems to have been the norm in Tibet. But the freedom to choose one's own course of religious practice did not mean—and should not be equated with—material ease and comfort. The life of the Tibetan *ani* in particular was not an easy one.[20]

It may be argued that the nun's order was never a strong component of Buddhism's development at any time or in any country.[21] Tibet was no exception. While the earliest ordination of Tibetan monks (a solemn ceremony in which the Indian Ācārya, Śāntirakṣita, ordained the first seven indigenous Tibetans at bSam-yas monastery in the late eighth century A.D.) is an event well documented and much lauded in the major religious annals of the country, I have been unable to find a single reference to the earliest ordination of Tibetan nuns. There were, however, *ani* in Tibet; and, though very few in number, there were even some *ani-mkhan-po-s*, or Abbesses. Thus for some Tibetan women, the life of a nun even with all its hardships, offered a viable, even attractive, means by which to practice their faith.

3.

Having presented the foregoing comments for reflection and clarification, I now turn to the specific case histories. As mentioned, I will here briefly summarize five different examples of nun's lives.

1. The Abbess of Sam-ding (bSam-sding) dgon-pa

bSam-sding was the State Nunnery of Tibet and its Abbess was regarded as the incarnation of the deity rDo-rje Phags-mo (*Skt.* Vajravārāhī). Situated seventy miles southwest of Lhasa, on a slip of land some 14,512 feet high and overlooking the famed Yam-dok (Yar-'brog) lake, the dgon-pa was a most impressive sight. Waddell mused that bSam-sding was "noteworthy as a monastery of monks as well as nuns, presided over by a female abbot."[22] He continued his description as follows:

> This august woman is known throughout Tibet as Dorje-P'ag-mo, or "the diamond sow"; the abbesses of Samding being held to be successive appearances in mortal form of the Indian goddess, Vajravarahi. The present incarnation of this goddess is thirty-three years old (in 1889); and is described as being a clever and capable woman, with some claim to good looks, and

> of noble birth. She bears the name of Nag-dban Rin-ch'en Kun-bzan-mo dbAn-mo, signifying "The most precious power of speech, the female energy of all good." Under this lady the reputation which Samding has long enjoyed for the good morals of both monks and nuns has been well maintained.[23]

Tucci's expedition briefly visited bSam-sding in 1948. In *To Lhasa and Beyond*, he comments:

> I could not leave the place without seeing the Samding monastery, built by Potopa Chogle Namgyal (P'yogs las rnam rgyal). That convent is famous on account of the incarnation of the goddess Dorjepamo (rDorje p'ag mo), "the hog-headed One" supposed to dwell there uninterruptedly changing [only] her mortal form. Never fear: the goddess' mortal mirror does not look that dreadful and was, at the time, a pretty girl of 13.[24]

The early nineteenth century Tibetan work, *The Geography of Tibet*, mentions bSam-sding dgon-pa and terms the Abbess a *rig-ma* (i.e. a "wisdom-being"; also a synonym for *mudrā*).[25] Both Taring[26] and Waddell[27] attribute the Abbess' high esteem to the fact that during the 1719 invasion of Tibet by the Dzungar Tartars she miraculously transformed herself and her followers into "a large herd of pigs"[28] whose sight caused the Dzungars to flee in disgust. The convent was chiefly affiliated with the rNying-ma sect, but its Abbess is the only woman in Tibet venerated on a par with and "accorded privileges shared only by" the Pan-chen and Dalai Lamas.[29]

2. *Ani Lochen*

In her wonderfully interesting autobiography, *Daughter of Tibet*, Rinchen Dolma Taring briefly mentions a saintly woman who commanded the respect of all the religious sects. This woman was called *Ani Lochen*. Sometimes a fuller title was given: "Shuksep Jetsun Lochen Rinpoche." Shuksep (*shugs-gseb—*

"Juniper Forest") named the location of Ani Lochen's nunnery, some thirty miles outside Lhasa. The titles "Jetsun" (*rje-btsun*) and "Rinpoche" are honorific ones, reserved for Tibet's most accomplished and treasured teachers.

Taring describes Ani Lochen as being the reincarnation[30] of Ma-gcig-lab-sgron-ma (mentioned previously),[31] and as also being affiliated primarily with the rNying-ma-pa sect. As a summary of Ani Lochen's life, Taring writes the following:

> She had been born in India in about 1820 at Tsopadma Rawalsar in the district of Mandi of a Nepalese mother and Tibetan father. From the age of six she preached, with a *thang-ka*, by singing of religion in a wonderfully melodious voice and whoever heard her found their hearts coming closer to religion. As a child she had a little goat to ride and when in her youth she went along the streets of Lhasa with her *thang-ka*, preaching from door to door, she caught the hearts of many Lhasa girls who became nuns and followed her. She was known as "Ani Lochen." . . . At the age of about forty Ani Lochen promised her mother that she would always stay in the mountains and meditate; later she found a place near Lhasa called Shuksep, where there was a cave in which Gyalwa Longchen Rabjampa had meditated. . . . Many nuns also came and there was a little nunnery nearby for about eighty women. People regularly visited Ani Lochen, for her cave was near Lhasa and she had many worshippers—lamas, monks, officials and women. Sometimes nuns would leave their nunnery to marry, but Ani Lochen always said, "Never mind—even if they have been nuns for only a week they will be different forever afterwards."[32]

There are differing accounts of this accomplished woman's age at death. At one place in *Daughter of Tibet*, Taring provides a photograph of Ani Lochen. Next to it the caption reads "Shuksep Jetsun Lochen Rinpoche, a saint. She died in 1950 aged over 130 years."[33] To my knowledge the only other source in English for information on Ani Lochen comes from Lobsang Lhalungpa.[34] Lhalungpa's comments regarding Ani Lochen are found in two separate sources. One says she died at age 115 years; the other says 113 years.

In an interview for *Parabola* magazine, Lhalungpa was asked about his own teachers. I give below excerpts of his response:

> Fortunately I have had quite a number of teachers. I was admitted to a monastery but my father wouldn't allow me to stay there; he wanted me to stay with him and study privately under great lamas. This I did. It proved to be very effective and beneficial to me. Some of them are still alive in India.
>
> I had a woman lama in Tibet, an extraordinary woman. Her name was Jetsun Lochen Rinpoche. She had very close connections with my family. Two of my cousins became nuns at her nunnery. It wasn't a nunnery in the strict sense of the word, but a kind of institution where old or young women—anyone—could go and spend time with her for different teachings, and then stay at the establishment and carry on their practices. There were many nuns and lay people as well. She belonged to the order known in the West as the Red Hat sect, the *Nyingmapa* order, but actually she was eclectic. In giving teachings to students or disciples, she would always speak in comparative terms and encourage them to develop understanding of every teaching of the different schools and traditions. She herself was certainly respected by all the great monasteries in Tibet; she was one of the most widely respected women teachers that have lived in Tibet.
>
> She lived to one hundred and fifteen years of age and had a tremendous following throughout the country. She never travelled very widely, but people came to her at her mountain retreat. An extraordinary woman! Not so much in terms of deep learning; while

> she knew a good deal about Buddhism itself, it was her own inner development, inner experience and attainment that was so great. A lot of people who didn't actually study with her still received from her directly. Just being present there in front of her, they seemed to experience some deep sort of change. . . .
>
> She never actually slept. She trained herself in that way. She was always in a high meditational state of mind—very alert. I was able to spend a good deal of time listening to her and she really gave me many things.
>
> I have had many great teachers, but this woman lama, Jetsun Lochen Rinpoche, gave me tremendous insight into the spiritual life.[35]

In his introductory "Chronicle" to the 1983 publication of *Tibet the Sacred Realm: Photographs 1880-1950*, Lhalungpa again speaks of Ani Lochen. In a section entitled "Teachings of the Great Lamas," he speaks of his education under Ling and Trijang Rinpoche(s) (the two chief tutors of the present Dalai Lama),[36] under Gonsartse Rinpoche, and lastly under Ani Lochen. In a sensitive portrayal, he states:

> Not long after that I went to visit a holy woman mystic named Jetsun Lochen at her nunnery in the Juniper Forest, thirty miles from Lhasa, in order to receive from her the highest esoteric teachings and initiations of the Nyingmapa order, known as Atiyoga. Her religious center was situated on the high slope of Mount Gangri Thokar (Whitehead Mountain), one of the most sacred places in Tibet. The only daughter of poor parents, Jetsun Lochen had shaped her own destiny in childhood. Showing intense interest in religious songs and studies, she had risen to the eminence of a revered lama. Long before I went to her, my family had been among her ardent followers. Some of my close relatives were nuns at the nunnery.
>
> During my first two-week visit I met with Jetsun

> Lochen for several hours a day, sometimes in the company of her main disciples. She was an extraordinary woman, small in stature, with a serene face radiating compassion and sensitivity. Only her white hair betrayed her age: she died a few years later at the age of one hundred thirteen. In her presence we felt an awesome power that permeated our whole stream-being. Her teachings and blessings have given me inner strength and inspiration ever since. To me she was the personification of the great woman teachers of Tibet.[37]

Taring notes that "Ani Lochen died in 1950, at the age of a hundred and thirty, and her reincarnation was born to Jigme's brother, Chime Dorje, in 1955. He was a fine little boy who remembered his prayers and many of his disciples, and he had just been recognized by the Dalai Lama as the true reincarnation when the uprising [i.e. of 1959] took place."[38] I do not know what has become of him.

3. and 4.: Two Ani-s of D'ing-ri

In the course of her description of D'ing-ri society (an area close to the Nepal-Tibet border where over a quarter of the hamlets are *ser-khyimdgon-pa*), Barbara Aziz gives brief portraits of two contemporary nuns. One is an "itinerant" nun named Ani Ch'o-dron, and the other a sort of hermit nun named Ani Drol-ma. I present these case histories as examples of living practitioners. Apart from my own oral history of Ani Dol-kar, Aziz's cases are the only published studies I have come across. Taken altogether, these three life histories vividly demonstrate the great flexibility of Tibetan religious and monastic life, the close ties and continual movement between village and *dgon-pa* and, importantly, the great varieties of religious practice that were commonplace and acceptable in pre-1959 Tibet.

Aziz introduces her account of Ani Ch'o-dron with the following general assessment:

> The escape from the hamlet to the *gon-pa* is usually the beginning of a new life for the refugee in one form or another. Those who realize they cannot remain in the *gon-pa* launch into an itinerant life from which they may never emerge. D'ing-ri is full of itinerants like A-ni Ch'o-dron and her son Zang-po. The son, now over fifty, only joined A-ni Ch'o-dron wandering around D'ing-ri after he broke his vow of celibacy and had to leave Dza-rong.[39]

Aziz's summary of Ani Ch'o-dron's life is described as follows:

> Chodon's pursuit began with the decisions she had to make after a poorly contracted marriage. "My family arranged it. They sent me far away to a house and village where I knew no one, not even my husband. And alone I had to bear the beatings his sister inflicted on my body. Because a baby started to grow inside my stomach, I stayed on to wait for this little companion. But two weeks after its arrival, the baby died," Chodron abruptly concluded, "and I went back to D'ing-ri."
>
> She described the first few years of her wanderings around D'ing-ri. Months were spent in the company of a band of itinerants—men and women who studied the texts and prayed together in abandoned retreats and moved through the mountains from one holy site to another. She confided that it only happened once that she lay with one of her companions. After that she returned home to the family of her brother, for she was pregnant with Zangpo. Until he was born Chodon lived on with her relatives. As soon as the boy was old enough to travel, the young mother took him with her back to the hermitages and pilgrims' paths.[40]

Introducing the case history of the retreatant nun, Ani Drolma, Aziz writes:

> Many small *gon-pa* around D'ing-ri are *a-nii-gon-pa*, annexes of the Tr'i-pon and Dza-rong systems. Here we find *a-ni* who prefer to remain near their home village and in touch with their kin. These local retreats also serve the aged members of the hamlets when they retire from domestic life and are too old to undergo any systematic training. . . . A-ni Drol-ma's history. . . . is another example of how one family's needs weave into the monastic and other religious life styles.[41]

And summarizing Ani Drol-ma's life, Aziz writes:

> Drol-ma had never wanted to marry, so before her approaching betrothal she had insisted on visiting Dza-rong and beginning her religious studies. Since her father's sister, Nam-drol, was already living at Dza-rong, this was easy to arrange. So Drol-ma, at the age of nineteen, went to live with her vestal aunt. She stayed at Dza-rong for a year until taking her own vestal vows to become what is known as a *rab-j'ang-a'ni*. A-ni Drol-ma thereupon left Dza-rong to return to Ku-ra village. For the next ten years she passed her time alternating between her home and the nearby sanctuary of J'ang-ding, an *an-nii-gon-pa* annexe of Dza-rong. Drol-ma says she had liked living with her brothers and their *na-ma*. She had also felt welcome there, and had not minded helping with domestic chores. The time came, however, when she found the growing children irritating, and Drol-ma left the house in preference for the quiet of the small *gon-pa*. It was a major move even though the retreat was not more than forty-five minutes away.
>
> Drol-ma took her youngest sister, then seventeen, with her to J'ang-ding. . . . Drol-ma became the girl's mentor [and] some months later they journeyed together to Dza-rong in order that the younger woman be ordained. So it was now two vowed nuns who

returned to J'ang-ding to live. They continued for two years, until the young nun became pregnant. This had happened when the girl was in Gang-gar visiting a married sister there. It was her sister's husband who had impregnated her—a stroke of luck for the family since the married sister had proved to be barren. That infertility was a greater shame than the young nun's apostacy. Therefore, as soon as the pregnant girl had made her amends to her *la-ma* and her other sister, she was welcomed as the junior wife in the Gang-gar house.

Meanwhile Drol-ma stayed on at J'ang-ding but it was not long before she built a hut at Dza-rong, making it her permanent home, and only returning to J'ang-ding during the unpleasant winters.[42]

5. *Ani Dol-kar (sGrol-dkar)*

Ani Lobsang Dol-kar is her religious ordination name. She considered telling me her given name prior to ordination, but then told me that she preferred if I "wrote down" only her religious name; that was sufficient and most important. I had spoken briefly with Ani Dol-kar a few times before showing up at her residence with my Uher tape recorder to interview her. She lived in a room of her own, in the house of her brother and his family.

She set the stage and tone of the interview by announcing that *before* we began, she would like to tell me why she had chosen to become a nun. She said:

> My parents gave me out in marriage to others and I gave birth to four children: two sons and two daughters. My first child, a son, was born when I was eighteen years old. He did not survive. I later had three other children—four altogether—but none of them lived. [Each of her children had died before reaching the age of two]. Then I prayed to *mGon-po* [i.e. Mahākāla] and asked many lamas about my fate; and I

> was told that "religion is very deep."

Apparently, it was at this time that Ani-Dol-kar had inquired about becoming a nun, for she next commented that:

> They [or he] said, "You think hard before becoming a nun. It is not an easy life. Think about whether you really want to do it. You have had no peace as a householder. You have suffered much. So, if you think you can really do it, becoming a nun is very good."

She then asked her husband, who gave his approval. Her husband was already a sick man. She said that she had told him, "If (or, as long as) you need me, I won't become a nun. When you don't need me, then I will become a nun!" "But then," she continued, "he died within a few months."

Ani Dol-kar was from Kyi-rong in Southwestern Tibet. Her "root guru" (Tib. *t'sa-ba'i bla-ma*) was one Chos-saṅs-rgyas Rinpoche, a bKa'-brgyud-pa hermit who preferred to do long retreats at the places in that area that were famed owing to their connection with Tibet's great yogi, Milarepa. Chos-saṅs-rgyas practiced meditation in caves and other isolated areas where Mila had practiced. Apparently, it was owing to Chos-saṅs-rgyas Rinpoche that Ani Dol-kar decided to become ordained. Since the Rinpoche had no monastery of his own, he suggested that she take ordination at the nearest monastic establishment so that the requisite quota of fully ordained monks could be assembled to administer to her the vows. The monastery happened to be a dGe-lugs-pa one named bSam-gtan-gling.[43] Unlike the portrayals of rigid distinctions between the sects found in many Western accounts of Tibetan religious life, the blending of traditions did not seem a problem for either Ani Dol-kar or her *guru*.

Further describing her teacher's advice, Dol-kar said:

> He told me not to enter the nunnery [there] since I had to take care of the children [i.e., her siblings, her father and mother having died since her marriage and she being the eldest of their six children]; but to go

> into retreat from time to time whenever I could. So I did whatever he advised me to do; no deviation from that!

Once ordained, Ani Dol-kar studied for a while at bSam-gtan-gling before returning home and later resuming her studies with Chos-saṅs-rgyas Rinpoche. Though she could not read, she described some of the teachings she had received orally. During her early tenure at bSam-gtan-gling she had had two teachers: Khensur Tenzin Dhondrup and Gelong Lobsang Tenpa. (Later in Tibet, Nepal, and India, she had taken teachings from the Dalai Lama and from both of his two chief tutors: Ling Rinpoche and Trijang Rinpoche. She had also studied with Rato, Tshenshap, and Kyab-rje Zong Rinpoche. She said it was impossible to list all her teachers.)

As for practicing, she had done many solitary retreats. She had managed to construct a small retreat hut for herself in relative nearness to her root *guru*. During such retreats, she had completed the *sngon-'gro* practices (100,000 prostrations and refuges, 100,000 *maṇḍala* offerings, 100,000 Vajrasattva *mantra* recitations, etc.) "Actually" she added, "I completed 200,000 of each of these; and I did more after coming to Nepal. In Tibet, because I had to take care of my brothers, I couldn't practice religion all the time; I had to stay home a lot. Since coming out of Tibet the kids have all grown up and I have no work [they now support her] so I keep on saying *maṇi*. But in Tibet, I would finish one *sngon-'gro* retreat, then return home to check on the family. Then another *sngon-'gro* retreat, then return home to check on the family. Then another *sngon-'gro* retreat, and then home again." Again, the fluid and continuous movement between domestic life and solitary religious practice was echoed in Ani Dol-kar's remarks.

When I suggested to Ani Dol-kar that there seemed to be far fewer nuns now than there had been in former times, she responded with a fascinating and somewhat curious—if not distorted(!)—account of the history of the Nun's Order. She said:

> Yes, very few, even when the Buddha himself was alive. It is said that Kun-dga'-ba [*Skt.* Ānanda] asked the Buddha to ordain a nun, so he ordained one. But because of this it is said that the Buddha's Dharma suffered much. Then rJe Rinpoche [i.e. Tsong-kha-pa, the founder of the dGe-lugs tradition into which Ani Dol-kar was ordained] offered a rite to the Buddha and "healed" the Buddha Dharma [in Tibet?]. So it is said.

I told her that some texts had said it was necessary to have a man's body in order to attain full enlightenment, and asked her opinion. She responded, "No one has a choice about his/her birth [or bodily] form. That may have been said during the Buddha's time but now anyone can practice, of course. It is only that we Tibetans are in other people's countries. It is difficult when one doesn't have freedom.[44] In Tibet there were thirty-eight nuns [belonging to the same group as those now in Yulmo, Nepal],[45] but only ten could come out. Some have [since] died; some couldn't earn a living, etc. . . . Women can get spoiled more easily than men; so in a way the Buddha had predicted [correctly] that women wouldn't be able to practice all of his teachings. So many times even his *dge-slong-ma* had to be restricted."

"But did that happen in Tibet as well?" I queried. 'Weren't there *dge-slong-ma-s* in Tibet?"

"That I don't know for sure. Probably not—there were some only during the Buddha's time."

Ani Dol-kar's final asessment of her religious career was stated as follows: "If I could practice higher thoughts and teachings, that would be better; but just saying OM MAṆI PADME HUṂ is enough for me. Even though I didn't learn how to read the scriptures and now have to content myself with simply reciting *maṇi*, by the grace of the Triple Gem [i.e., *Buddha*, *Dharma*, and *Saṅgha*], my mind is happy."

* * *

The nuns' lives recounted above mirrored the lives of hundreds, even thousands like themselves in Tibet. They moved in a dynamic and vital religious world both extraordinary and commonplace. In terms of religious practice they chose and changed courses until a balance was found which suited their own individual needs, abilities and aspirations. Such flexibility and dynamism is missed (or worse, condemned) by Westerners who approach Tibetan Buddhism with preconceived and static ideas about what constitutes the sanctity of the religious life.

In closing, let me again quote a few passages from Aziz. In *Tibetan Frontier Families*, characterizing both the day-to-day happenings in a Tibetan *dgon-pa* and the flexible nature of Tibetan Buddhist religious life in general, she wrote:

> In *Views From The Monastery Kitchen* (1976) I make a point of illustrating the open, accommodating and flexible atmosphere of the Tibetan *gon-pa*. One meets here several individuals, lay and cleric, men and women, each of whom is a distinctive personality with a role in the community suited to them. There are few *ch'o-pa* who live in a silent retreat meditating, reading and writing for months and years on end.
>
> Most *ch'o-pa* I have met are not so inspired, or so disciplined, or so economically independent. They begin their religious training learning simple vocal and bodily exercises, performing simple rituals and reading. For many this is the extent of their religious education. The few inclined to scholarship, debate and liturgy are brought into the inner circle of *gon-pa* offices and given the most rigorous training. The rest keep employed in numerous menial tasks around the *gon-pa* kitchen performing those minimal but useful religious exercises.[46]

And again:

> A peculiarity of this system is its ability to develop the

> individual rather than simply mould him into a member of a rigid community. I have been surprised to find that the *gon-pa* does not subsume the needs of the individual. Here more than in the hamlet one finds men and women leading rich, individualistic lives. If one has the opportunity to meet and talk with *ch'o-pa* one quickly realizes that each is a different person who interprets his religion in a particular way and expects of it something unique.[47]

In Tibet, as in all other countries and historical periods, people practice religion; and whether monks or nuns, people are as varied as any other species. Perhaps with more communication and dialogue with Tibetans we in the West can come nearer to a understanding of the varied features of Tibetan religious life, as practiced and lived; and to an appreciation of the benefits of its "open and accommodating atmosphere." Perhaps we shall even ourselves become more open and accommodating by virtue of the attempt.

7. *Tibetan Nuns and Nunneries*

Karma Lekshe Tsomo

In descriptions of Tibet and Tibetans, monks have figured prominently and a wealth of detailed information is available on their way of life. It is also well known that the religious life was open to women, yet little is known of the numbers and circumstances of the women who opted for monastic life. Many historical accounts mention the lives of accomplished nuns in Tibet, but there are few in-depth reports on their lifestyle and spiritual practice. The present survey attempts to serve as a background to understanding the situation of Tibetan nuns today.

NUNS IN TIBET

By dint of comparison to the enormous number of monks and monasteries for monks that existed in Tibet before the communist invasion of 1950-59, the number of nuns and monasteries for nuns has been underestimated. Statistics gathered recently by the Council for Religious and Cultural Affairs of His Holiness the Dalai Lama, Dharamsala, reveal that the number of nuns and nunneries in Tibet prior to the events of 1959 was quite significant. These findings indicate a total number of 618 nunneries in the various traditions, of which 290 were rNying-ma, 160 dGe-lugs, 128 bKa'-brgyud and 40 Sa-skya. There were 7141 nuns residing in rNying-ma nunneries, 6831 in dGe-lugs, 3697 in bKa'-brgyud and 1159 in Sa-skya—a total of 18,828 nuns altogether, making Tibet the home of one of the largest communities of Buddhist nuns in the world. (There are no records of nunneries belonging to the Bon tradition.)

Nunneries were found throughout the length and breadth of Tibet. Many were situated in remote, isolated locations, but there were also more than ten nunneries located in and around the Lhasa area. Of the 618 nunneries reported above, 271 were of considerable size, housing more than thirty nuns each. Some 40 of these were extensive, with more than 100 nuns in residence.[1] The largest reported was the bKa'-brgyud nunnery known as dGe-chak Thek-chen-gling in the Nang-chen district of Eastern Tibet with 1000 nuns. A dGe-lugs nunnery known as sByor-dge sGrol-ri Zhabs-gon bTzun-dGon, housing over 600 nuns, was located in the Brag-gyab region of Eastern Tibet. Functioning nunneries of such size are unknown in other Buddhist countries.

For the most part, monasteries for men and those for women were distinctly separate in Tibet. In exceptional cases, particularly in the rNying-ma tradition, communities of monks and nuns would be located nearby one another, studying together with the same teacher and gathering for ceremonies in a common assembly all. There were also cases of nuns staying in retreat communities or in caves with one or two nuns as companions; others stayed with relatives who provided them with the daily necessities, leaving them free to attend to their spiritual practice.

In their daily lives, the nuns concentrated on *dharma* practice consisting of study, chanting and meditation. Except for those engaged in strict retreat, each resident also took a share of the responsibility for the maintenance and functioning of the nunnery. The chief administrator was generally a nun selected from among their own number and designated Abbess (*mkhen-mo*), but could also be a respected monk who served as chief instructor in the scriptures and was termed the Abbot (*mkhen po*). The chief scripture teacher for the nunnery as a whole could also be the nun most learned in the texts. Education in fundamental subjects such as reading and writing was normally provided on an individual basis with senior nuns taking responsibility for two or three students. A great deal of emphasis was placed on the memorization of texts, with less attention given to mastering the philosophical topics that are normally undertaken by Tibetan monks. Lacking opportunities for higher studies in philosophy, fewer nuns became qualified as instructors, tending to devote themselves chiefly to meditation and liturgical practices instead.

Interestingly enough, one of the most famous nuns in Tibetan history was not Tibetan at all, but rather Indian. This is the renowned dge-slong-ma dPal-mo. Previously an Indian princess known as Lakṣmi who was afflicted with leprosy, she became the original progenitor of the fasting practice (*nyung-gnas*) of Avalokiteśvara (sPyan-ras-gzigs), having received blessings from the great *Bodhisattva* directly through her meditation. She was known as a great *siddha* and her story is still frequently told in connection with this fasting ritual which is especially popular among Tibetan nuns. Though the biographies make it sound as if she visited Tibet, there is no conclusive evidence to support this. Nevertheless, it is certain that she travelled to Nepal and transmitted certain lineages to Tibetans there. The lineage of Mahākarunika transmitted by Atīśa in Tibet is also traced to her.[2]

Although dGe-slong-ma dPal-mo was fully ordained as a *bhikṣuni*, it appears that she was unable to transmit the *bhikṣuni* lineage to Tibet. The *Vinaya* texts require that a complete *Bhikṣuni Saṅgha* be present in order to administer the full ordination. In the Mulasarvāstivādin tradition followed by Tibetans, this consists of twelve nuns: a precept master (*mkhen-mo*), and instructress (*slob-dpon-ma*), and ten more nuns, all of whom must be *bhikṣuni-s*. The ordination must be conducted by the *Bhikṣuni Saṅgha* first, then confirmed the same day by a *Bhikṣu Saṅgha* composed of no fewer than ten fully ordained monks. It would seem that the requisite number of *bhikṣuni-s* were not available to participate in this elaborate ordination procedure. As a consequence, the *bhikṣuni* lineage was never transmitted to Tibet. Nuns there normally received thirty-six precepts and practiced their whole lives as novices (*śrāmaṇerikās*). There were also a large number of women who shaved their heads and lived as nuns without receiving formal ordination as a *śrāmaṇerikā*. Women who became ordained later in life, after having raised families, were referred to as "senior practitioners" (*rgan-chos*).

There is a section in *The Blue Annals* that describes twenty-four female disciples of Pha Dam-pa Saṅs-rgyas (eleventh century A.D.) as nuns, but does not give specific details about the ordination and precepts they held.[3] Many miraculous occurrences are narrated in connection with these female practitioners, including relics and rainbows appearing at the time of death. The auspicious signs that appeared in relation to their meditation practice indicate that many of them were *ḍākinī-s* (*mkha' 'gro*), meaning emanations of enlightened mind in female form. Though many of them achieved spiritual realization without fanfare and applause, women of insight such as these appeared frequently in Tibetan history even up to recent times.

The nun of highest rank in Tibet was bSam-sding rDo-rje Phags-mo, residing in bSam-sding-dgon, one day's ride from Lhasa. Successive incarnations were recognized as embodiments of the deity Vajravārāhī and accorded high respect. The incarnate who lived in the early half of this century is said to have counted a large number of monks among her disciples. Her successor was chosen by the Chinese and was not the Tibetan's preferred candidate. She is currently playing a role in the communist government and does not take much interest in religious matters.

Another well-known nun in recent Tibetan history was

known as Shuksep Jetsun Lochen Rinpoche. Born around 1820 in Rewalsar, India, at the Lotus Lake (mTso-pad-ma) reputed to be the birthplace of Guru Padmasambhava, she was said to be an incarnation of Ma-gcig-lab-sgron-ma, a famous Tibetan *yoginī* of the eleventh century. She became well-loved for singing religious ballads, being revered for her meditation and knowledge of the scriptures as well. She lived to be well over one hundred years old and is remembered by Tibetans who met her during the early half of this century.[4]

Indisputably, the religious life was open to women as well as to men in Tibet, as the above examples illustrate. However, there were social and biological factors that resulted in fewer women than men joining the order. Though Tibetan women enjoyed a greater measure of freedom than their sisters in other traditional Asian societies, the social structure was nonetheless decidedly patriarchal. Even while wielding a considerable amount of power in household affairs and commercial activities, women tended to accept roles as wives and mothers in accordance with the wishes of their parents. Marriages were usually arranged, be it with the consent of the principles, and society preferred to see women demure and in domestic roles. Even a girl of strong spiritual inclinations would not routinely be encouraged by her family to take up the monastic life, whereas a boy of similar disposition would surely be placed in a monastery with pride. In addition, the physical risks of child-bearing in the Tibetan climate, combined with a lack of taboos against remarriage, may have resulted in a demand for women and a reluctance to see them lead celibate lives.

In theory, religious practice by men and women was regarded as equally praiseworthy, but in reality a subtle tendency developed to place greater value on the efforts of men in spiritual matters. While enlightenment is available to men and women without discrimination in the Buddhist view, there exist prayers of supplication which give the distinct impression that a male rebirth is preferable to that of a female. Certain passages in the Buddhist texts enumerating the faults of women were addressed to monks in praise of celibacy, but can function to erode women's self-image if quoted out of context. I have spoken with Tibetan women who, on the one hand regret having made prayers for a male rebirth when they were children, yet who have not gained confidence enough to pray for a female rebirth. They still cite the disadvantages of enforced dependence and vulnerability to pregnancy as making the female state less desirable both from the worldly and religious points of view. Women even today are seen as requiring more protection and entitled to less personal freedom than men. These factors may mitigate against a decision to take up the ordained life and help explain why fewer women than men entered religious communities.

TIBETAN NUNS IN EXILE

The number of nuns who have managed to escape from Tibet since 1959, either individually or in small groups, is hard to determine precisely. In fact, the migration to religious freedom in India and Nepal continues even today. Many of the original refugees succumbed to the difficulties of the journey or have died subsequently. Numerous other women have received ordination while living in exile. There are an estimated 900 nuns of the Tibetan tradition in India and Nepal today.

In the early years of exile, nuns lived isolated lives, some being cared for by relatives and others being forced to take up road construction or child care in order to sustain themselves. Some nuns gradually settled in communities together in an attempt to preserve their religious traditions. Today an increasing number of nunneries are developing as a result of women's interest in the monastic life.

Among the more than three hundred Buddhist monastic communities reported in India, several house nuns practicing in the Tibetan tradition. The largest of these nunneries are inhabited primarily by Tibetan refugee nuns. Other smaller nunneries are found in Ladakh, Zanskar, Nepal, and Bhutan. The present survey concerns the lifestyle, living conditions and educational facilities in several Tibetan refugee nunneries in India and Nepal.

Geden Choeling Nunnery

Geden Choeling is the largest Tibetan nunnery in India and probably the largest functioning nunnery of the Tibetan tradition in the world, since most of the nunneries in Tibet itself have been destroyed and are no longer operational. It is located in a lovely wooded area near Macleod Ganj in Dharamsala, Himachal Pradesh, and has an enrollment of eighty nuns. Sixty of these are accommodated on the grounds, while the remaining nuns live with relatives or on their own in the village nearby, gathering at the nunnery for ceremonies and special teachings.

The majority of the nuns at Geden Choeling are Tibetan. There is also a large representation of nuns who are ethnically Tibetan, but whose homelands are mountain areas which are politically Indian, such as Lahul, Spiti, Kinnaur, Zanskar, and Ladakh. Since their language and customs are closely related, they fit into Tibetan communities very easily. Because of the developing study program at this nunnery and its proximity to the residence of His Holiness the Dalai Lama, with access to his teachings and blessings, dozens of nuns from these areas are anxious to be admitted here.

There is currently an influx of nuns newly-arrived from Tibet, which has intensified housing demands at the existing nunneries. Arriving from Tibet with little more than the clothes on their backs, these nuns have high expectations for pursuing the *dharma* in India. Seeing their poverty and sincerity, Geden Choeling has made special provisions to admit eleven of these newcomers in the last year and is putting them up in two overcrowded classrooms.

The residents of this nunnery are generally young, most being under thirty. In recent years, due to the scarcity of accommodations, admissions have been restricted to application in the lower age brackets. Another factor in this decision is that the young nuns are more capable of assuming their share of the work load, often possessing such useful skills as accounting, sewing, language fluency (Hindi, English, Nepali), and so forth. The majority of the responsibility for maintaining the nunnery is shouldered by the nuns themselves, who share in the cooking, cleaning, shopping, building construction, and whatever tasks are necessary. The trend in Tibetan nunneries is toward self-sufficiency.

About three years ago, the nuns of Geden Choeling began to take an active interest in pursuing the study curriculum undertaken by monks in the great monastic universities. They took the initiative of seeking out a teacher in the village to instruct them in the basic logic texts. The younger nuns have displayed a keen interest in improving their learning opportunities and even the senior nuns are increasingly realizing the value of improved education for ordained women.

As the interest and numbers of the students grew, a senior student from the nearby Institute of Buddhist Dialectics was selected to teach the text *Collected Topics (bsDus-grva)* at the nunnery itself and time periods for debating sessions were allotted. Although the logic texts are very technical and profound, and generally their study has been deemed the prerogative of male scholars, the nuns have shown tremendous aptitude and great enthusiasm in this unique field of learning.

The daily schedule of the nuns begins with chanting at 6:00 A.M., after which a breakfast of tea and bread is served. There is a short break during which individual and communal living areas are swept. Following this, classes in the logic texts are held at both beginning and intermediate levels. From 10:00 to 11:30 A.M. is the morning debate session, followed by a communal lunch consisting of rice or steamed buns with *dahl* (lentil soup), potatoes, or vegetables. In accordance with Buddhist monastic discipline, no evening meal is served, but a nun may save half of her lunch to eat in the evening if she wishes. There is a rest period after lunch until grammar class convenes at 2:00 P.M. Following this, younger nuns study handwriting, Tibetan grammar at the beginning level, and reading with senior nuns who are assigned to them as teachers. After classes, afternoon tea is served and the nuns have time to study on their own until the evening debate session begins.

Already a second logic class has been started to meet the needs of recent entrants and a second teacher has been engaged to teach it. The senior class is currently studying *Logical Reasoning* (*rTags-rig*); subsequent to this they will begin a seven-year course in the *Perfection of Wisdom* texts (*Phar-phyin*). Most of their studies revolve around the basic philosophical texts, but there are also many texts and prayers that are traditionally learned by memory among Tibetans. Each day, a nun takes up a certain number of lines for memorization and recites them in the evening before the senior nun who serves as her teacher. To retain previously memorized material also requires frequent recitation and the nuns can often be heard until as late as midnight reciting the texts aloud in the surrounding forest.

Although the daily schedule outlined above is generally adhered to, it is punctuated by special teachings and other occasions for assembly (*tsogs*), including prayers, rituals, and recitation of texts. These are requested by various members of the lay community and donations are offered to cover expenses. Such religious activities are valued as methods of practice which accumulate great merit and are considered to have particular efficacy in removing obstacles for the sponsor as well as for the practitioners themselves. The donations offered by the sponsors for these ceremonies comprise a substantial portion of the nunnery's income. The nuns may also be offered a few rupees each as a personal donation to be used for buying soap, clothes, and other necessities. While almost everyone has faith in the value of these practices, they do tend to interfere with the study program, particularly when they extend over many days or weeks.

In the decade since its inception, Geden Choeling has developed into an important practice and learning center, clearly reflecting the heartfelt longing of women to engage in intensive *dharma* practice. As educational opportunities open up and living conditions improve, more and more qualified young women are inevitably being drawn to monastic life. The present nunnery has expanded so rapidly that it has far outgrown its existing facilities. Not only is living space totally inadequate; the prayer hall, classrooms, kitchen and sanitation requirements have all been eclipsed. Long-range goals include improvements in the study program and expansion of existing facilities to accommodate twenty aspiring applicants who wish to join in the life of the community.

Mahayana Buddhist Nunnery

The Mahayana Buddhist Nunnery was first established in Dalhousie by an English *bhikṣuni*, Ven. Khechok Palmo (Freda Bedi). Some time later a site became available in Tilokpur, midway between Dharamsala and the nearest rail junction, Pathankot. The great saint and tantric adept Tilopa is said to have meditated here, and indeed, the place seems to have a very special atmosphere, with unusual rock formations, a Hindu temple, and several unique caves. The nunnery is set on a bluff overlooking the caves, somewhat apart from the local Indian village.

There are fifty nuns enrolled here, ranging in age from seven to seventy-three. They hail from places as distant as Assam, Kinnaur, Mundgod, and of course, Tibet. Most are between the ages of twenty and thirty; many are orphans or semi-orphans. The nuns follow the traditions of the Karma Kagyu school, specializing in ritual and meditation. They have appointed as Abbess one of their own nuns, Karma Hosey, who received a *shastri* degree from the Institute of Higher Tibetan Studies in Sarnath, and look to H. E. Situ Rinpoche as their spiritual advisor. There is no resident teacher or formal study program at the moment, though there are hopes for developing one. In the meanwhile, senior nuns serve as teachers to the younger ones and teachings are received periodically from visiting Lamas.

The nuns of Tilokpur are well-known for their excellent practice, specializing in rituals to Tara, Mahakala, and other meditational deities. They continue these practices daily, whether or not a sponsor requests them. They rise at 4:00 each morning, and frequently engage in the fasting ritual of Avalokiteśvara, a practice which may last many days at a time. The nuns are very sincere in their practice and radiate a warmth that immediately communicates to visitors. There is a small guest-house on a slope below the nunnery, where visitors are welcome to stay briefly or for extended retreats. The site is very conducive to meditation practice.

Most of the nuns are between the ages of twenty and thirty, with three under the age of ten. They are very enterprising, doing most of the building and repair work of their facilities themselves. They take turns attending teachings and important ceremonies that are held in nearby Dharamsala. Several of the young nuns are pursuing their education in the Tibetan Central Schools, returning to the nunnery for holidays. The general subjects they study will give them valuable skills which will be an asset to the nunnery in the future. One of the nuns is currently enrolled at the Institute for Higher Tibetan Studies in Sarnath, one is studying to become a doctor at the Tibetan Medical Institute in Dharamsala, and several others have also expressed an interest in receiving higher education. Two have gone abroad to serve as translators, one to Sweden and another to Hong Kong.

Perhaps reflecting the spirit of their English founder, the nuns show a great deal of inner strength and initiative in their *dharma* practice. Even when not engaged in the fasting practice (*nyung-gnas*), the daily schedule at Tilokpur often includes taking the twenty-four-hour Mahāyāna precepts (*thek-chen-gso-sbyong*), which preclude breakfast and supper. During the day, intensive practice is pursued with a minimum of conversation and a maximum of mindfulness. The nuns are skilled in ritual and adept in performing a wide range of ceremonies, including the construction of offerings and playing of all the ritual instruments. All residents participate in a rotating schedule of kitchen, maintenance and managerial duties, serving for terms of one to three years. Everyone takes part on an equal basis and the community functions smoothly and harmoniously. The nunnery currently has eight nuns engaged in the traditional three-year retreat at a site near Bir. This is the first three-year group retreat for women to be held in India and one of the few in history. When the first group completes the retreat in early 1988, a second group will be selected on the basis of seniority and another retreat will begin. Three nuns are chosen to serve the retreat participants on a rotating basis by cooking, shopping, and so forth. The intensive practice being undertaken at this retreat site will undoubtedly produce a number of highly-qualified meditation instructors who will be able to serve as role models and teachers to other women in the future.

The first Tibetan nuns to receive full ordination are members of this nunnery. In 1984, four nuns travelled to Hong Kong to participate in the *bhikṣuni* ordination held at Po Lin Monastery. In a 45-day ceremony, they received the 348 *bhikṣuni* precepts enumerated in the Dharmagupta school of *Vinaya*, the ten major and forty-eight minor *bodhisattva* precepts detailed in the *Brahmajāla Sūtra* of the Chinese tradition, as well as rigorous training in discipline and deportment. Six more nuns attended the ordination ceremony held at the same monastery in October/November of 1987; these included two Tibetan refugees, one Sikkimese, one Bhutanese, one nun from the Kinnaur district of India, and one from the Mon people who live in Arunachal Pradesh, eastern India. It is hoped that a strong *Bhikṣuni Saṅgha* will gradually be established within the Tibetan tradition which will revive this ancient order in India after a lapse of nearly one thousand years.

Plans for enlarging the nunnery and expanding existing facilities have been drawn up. These plans are ambitious, but there is a tremendous need to make space for the large numbers of women who are anxious to devote themselves full-time to spiritual development. Nuns newly arrived from Tibet and applicants from Himālayan border areas are being turned away due to a lack of accommodations. The present residents would be happy to admit newcomers, for they see the virtue of a large vigorous community, but they are hampered by insufficient living space. In the meantime, applicants are being put on a waiting list until space becomes available.

Keydong Thukche Choeling

Keydong Thukche Choeling Nunnery was originally located in the sKyid-grong region of Tibet. After being forced to flee in 1959, the nuns relocated in the high mountains of Nepal. Sadly, their tribulations were not over; some years later, the nunnery was washed away in a flash flood. The nuns had all gone to attend the observances commemorating H. H. the Dalai Lama's birthday in a nearby village and returned in the evening to find that not a shred of the buildings or their possessions had been spared. Owning nothing but the clothes in which they stood, they began from scratch to collect donations towards re-establishing the nunnery. Eventually, they were able to acquire a small piece of property behind the sacred site of Swayambhu in the Kathmandu Valley.

There are currently forty-one nuns enrolled at Thukche Choeling, the majority being under twenty years of age. One nun, twenty-three years old, handles the majority of correspondence and teaches English to the others. The administrative tasks are handled by a committee of four senior nuns who assume responsibility for the functioning of the nunnery. These nuns are very capable, attending to their duties with a cheerful and conscientious attitude.

The day begins at 4:30 A.M. with prayers to the female protective deity Tara which last until 8:00 A.M. Classes in the basic logic texts are held until time for lunch, which consists of rice, *dahl* and vegetables. After lunch there are classes in English and Tibetan grammar throughout the afternoon, with further recitation of Tara prayers until supper at 6:00 P.M. Sessions are regularly scheduled for debating the text studied in the morning, while evenings are reserved for independent study and memorization of the scriptures.

The nuns in charge are especially interested in seeing the nunnery develop into a learning center for training young women in Tibetan language and religious texts. A teacher is in residence to instruct the younger nuns in recitation, grammar, handwriting, and general Buddhist tenets. Another qualified teacher comes regularly from outside to instruct the nuns in the basic logic texts and the techniques used for debating them. The nuns are eager to engage in these studies on a par with the monks in the great monastic universities. They fully understand the value of education for young people in Buddhism.

There are many women who would like to take advantage of such a study program, including large numbers of new nuns coming into Nepal from Tibet who are destitute and urgently need a place to settle. Plans are being drawn up to construct a prayer hall, classrooms, and additional living quarters since present facilities are totally inadequate. The senior nuns are hoping that a program for expansion will get underway before they are too old to supervise it, as the majority of the nuns are too young to take responsibility for the building plans.

Samten Choeling Nunnery

Samten Choeling is closely affiliated with the Nyingma Buddhist Monastery at Panggaon Cave near Manali and is under the spiritual direction of Ven. Khenpo Thupten, a monk-scholar of the Nyingma tradition. There are thirty-eight nuns in residence here, the majority being between twenty and forty years of age. They live on the face of a rocky cliff in simple houses which they have built themselves of stones and mud. Occasionally, when there is a sponsor, the monks and nuns gather together for a particular ceremony and eat communally. Otherwise, the nuns each cook individually and are responsible for their own maintenance. They manage this with help from family and friends who offer donations of money and supplies.

The annual schedule is divided into a term of studies during the summer months and a period for independent retreats during the winter months. The rainy season retreat during summer is a time of intensive teachings when residents make a vow not to leave the premises for three months. Despite the very simple facilities, the nuns enjoy the isolated location which they find ideal for concentrated *dharma* practice. When an entrant first arrives and wishes to build a new retreat house, she need only gather the building materials and supply others in the community with food for a week or two while they help with the building. Since stones and mud are available locally, this makes the cost of construction quite reasonable.

Khenpo Thupten serves as teacher of both meditation and scriptures, placing emphasis on Indian texts and classics of the Nyingma tradition. During the study term there are three classes held each day in various subjects. There are plans to expand the curriculum as living conditions improve and sufficient textbooks become available. The nuns' aim is to achieve a healthy balance of Buddhist studies and actual meditation experience.

Jangchub Choeling Nunnery

Jangchub Choeling is a new project for the development of a learning center for nuns in south India. The concept is to provide a course of training in philosophical studies equivalent to that traditionally undertaken by monks in the great monastic universities of Drepung, Ganden and Sera. Located in the Tibetan refugee settlement of Mundgod, this project has received official backing from the local representative of the Tibetan Government-in-Exile and help from the Tibetan Women's Association. A large prayer hall has been constructed and a building previously belonging to the old people's home next door has been renovated as a hostel for the student nuns.

Thus far, the nunnery has thirty-seven nuns enrolled, most of whom are below the age of twenty. At the moment the younger nuns are continuing classes in the settlement's day school and taking up Buddhist studies in the afternoons. A senior nun, Thubten Lhatso, has been appointed as teacher, also serving as coordinator of religious activities. She tutors the young nuns in reading, writing, chanting and calligraphy. There are plans to institute a program of studies in the basic logic texts beginning in 1988. Instructors can be invited from the Drepung and Ganden monasteries which have been re-established in exile and are situated nearby. It is hoped that a model educational program can be implemented which will attract talented young women to higher Buddhist studies and provide them opportunities for developing as teachers of the philosophical texts in the future.

Khachoe Ghakyil Nunnery

Khachoe Ghakyil is a community of twenty-one nuns, most of them newly arrived from Tibet, which has grown up in association with Kopan Monastery near Kathmandu, Nepal. It is under the spiritual direction of Ven. Thubten Zopa Rinpoche, with administrative duties being handled by Thubten Tse-yang, a twenty-nine-year-old nun who has been trained as a translator.

The nuns currently occupy monastery housing and have access to all the programs and facilities available to the monks. They take part in a full curriculum which includes Tibetan grammar, English, Buddhist texts, and debating. The nuns are enthusiastic in their studies and practice, also contributing their share to the practical functioning of the community. However, existing facilities are overcrowded and the time has come for the nunnery to develop independently.

The ideal solution is to procure land in the vicinity for the establishment of a monastic community especially for women. There are plans to develop the nunnery as a study center in response to the needs of nuns recently arrived from Tibet who wish to take up a serious study of Buddhist philosophy. Teachers can be invited from Kopan monastery to give instruction in logic, as well as ritual and meditation. The nuns are anxious to evolve a program on their own which will be geared to their particular interests, at the same time preparing them to help preserve Tibet's unique religious culture.

CONCLUSION

For years Tibetan nuns have been somewhat disadvantaged, in that religious life tended to center around communities of monks. Being quite humble and self-effacing by nature, nuns have remained quietly in the background and continued their practices in solitude. Study of higher philosophical texts became primarily the domain of male scholars, and religious education for women was somewhat neglected. Having little access to facilities for such higher studies, women lost faith in their intellectual capabilities, turning to meditation and other practices instead. In these they excelled, and there are numerous references to highly realized female practitioners in Tibetan historical sources. Still, due to cultural conditioning, social expectations, and their own delusions of incapability, the range of religious opportunities for women was far more limited than for men. These limitations were most substantially felt in the area of education.

In the last decade, much progress has been made in reversing and mitigating these disadvantages. In India, young Tibetan women receive public education up to the high school level on an equal par with young men. A large number have gone on to university, later entering the teaching and other professions. The quality of religious education for women has improved, but there is much more progress to be made. Intelligent young women who are inclined toward monastic life need to be encouraged and facilities at the nunneries need to be expanded to accommodate them. Education in the nunneries needs to be established and systematically organized to provide instruction in both religious and secular fields. Nuns and other young women need incentives for pursuing higher education at universities to qualify them as teachers so that they may take up positions to benefit other women as well as society at large. Changes are currently underway that will assure Tibetan women a greater role in religious and cultural life.

Notes

CHAPTER ONE: YESHE TSOGYEL

1. Keith Dowman, tr., *Sky Dancer: The Secret Life and Songs of the Lady Yeshe Tsogyel* (London: Routledge and Kegan Paul, 1984) and Tarthang Tulku, tr., *Mother of Knowledge: The Enlightenment of Ye-shes mTsho-rgyal* (Oakland: Dharma Press, 1983).

2. The most well-known source for this basic mythic motif is Joseph Campbell, *The Hero With a Thousand Faces* (Cleveland and New York: World Publishing Company, 1956).

3. This terminology is used to distinguish the two levels often found in Tibetan narratives. The more exoteric level of the story can well be handled by the term "myth" as used in history of religions. But it is helpful to have another term to distinguish the same story, being told from another level or from another point of view. Some use the term "sacred history," though there is no consensus as yet.

4. Tarthang Tulku, pp. xi-xii.

5. *Ibid.*, p. 13.

6. *Ibid.*, p. 5; Dowman, p. 3. This passage discusses Tsogyel from the ultimate point of view by discussing her ultimate ex-

istence in terms of the *trikāya*, the three bodies of the Buddha. A good discussion of this difficult concept is found in Bhikshu Sangharakshita, *A Survey of Buddhism* (Boulder: Shambhala, 1980), pp. 240-255. Relatively detailed information about Vajrayoginī can be obtained in Chogyam Trungpa, "Sacred Outlook: The Vajrayoginī Shrine and Practice," in *The Silk Route and the Diamond Path: Esoteric Buddhist Art on the Trans-Himalayan Trade Routes*, ed. Deborah E. Klimburg-Salter.

7. Tarthang Tulku, p. 12.
8. *Ibid.*, p. 7.
9. *Ibid.*, p. 7.
10. *Ibid.*, p. 13.
11. Dowman, p. 10.
12. *Ibid.*, p. 16.
13. *Ibid.*, p. 44.
14. *Ibid.*, p. 78.
15. *Ibid.*, p. 85.
16. *Ibid.*, p. 86.
17. *Ibid.*, p. 89.
18. *Ibid.*, p. 92.
19. "Terma" texts are especially known or important in the more esoteric forms of Tibetan Buddhism. Supposedly, recognizing the need for them in future ages, great teachers encode the appropriate messages and hide them. Later, they are mystically rediscovered by another great teacher and taught much more widely by him or her. This concept could be compared to the stories found already in the beginnings of Mahāyāna, to the effect that the Śākyamuni Buddha taught the Mahāyāna *sūtras* during his own historical life but then hid them with the *nāga-s* when he realized people were not yet ready to hear them. Both stories, on one level of analysis, function to show that "new" religious developments and texts are not really deviations.
20. Dowman, p. 125.
21. This term and the stories narrated at this point seem connected with the Mahāyāna emphasis on compassion, and

to be examples of perfected *tong-len* practice. As a meditation practice, on the medium of the breath, one gives away all one's positive experience and qualities to others and then takes on their negativity and suffering. The fact that Tsogyel takes on these experiences as her "final austerity" and really is able to relieve the suffering of others *after* years of intense Vajrayāna practice demonstrates an important and often missed point about the Vajrayāna—it is an *upāya*, the skillful means quickly to attain the Mahāyāna so as to manifest Buddha-activity in the world.

22. Dowman, p. 135.

23. *Ibid.*, p. 146.

24. "*Bardo*" is the intermediate period between death and taking on a new body at conception. It is said to be extremely confusing and frightening to those of small attainments. For a translation and commentary on the classic text about the *bardo*, see Francesca Fremantle and Chogyam Trungpa, trs., *The Tibetan Book of the Dead: The Great Liberation Through Hearing in the Bardo* (Boulder and London: Shambhala, 1975).

25. Dowman, p. 147.

26. *Ibid.*, p. 150.

27. *Ibid.*, p. 186.

28. *Ibid.*, p. 26.

29. *Ibid.*, p. 26.

30. *Ibid.*, p. 44.

31. *Ibid.*, pp. 118-119.

32. *Ibid.*, p. 56.

33. *Ibid.*, p. 147.

34. *Ibid.*, p. 150.

35. *Ibid.*, pp. 122-124. Bracketed phrase borrowed from Tarthang Tulku's translation of the same passage, p. 145.

36. A full discussion of the feminine and masculine principles in Vajrayāna Buddhism would be a vast undertaking, especially since much of the material is part of the esoteric teachings. My statement here summarizes my article "The Feminine Principle in Tibetan Vajrayāna Buddhism: Reflections of A Buddhist Feminist," *Journal of Transpersonal Psychology*, vol.

16, no. 3 (1984): pp. 179-192.

37. The term "vision quest" comes from the Native American traditions. It refers to an initiation in which young people go out alone to "cry for vision from the other world." It also refers, more metaphorically, to the life-long quest for a deeper vision of reality. For a short, beautiful, and authentic first-person narrative of a vision quest, see Arthur Amiotte, "Eagles Fly Over," *Parabola: Myth and the Quest for Meaning*, vol. 1, no. 3 (Sept. 1976): pp. 28-41.

38. Extensive hagiographic literature now is found in translation. The only other text addressed specifically to the hagiography of women is Tsultrim Allione's *Women of Wisdom* (London: Routledge and Kegan Paul, 1984). Padmasambhava's life story, traditionally attributed to Yeshe Tsogyel is translated as *The Life and Liberation of Padmasambhava* (Berkeley: Dharma Publishing Co., 1978). Other important biographies include Herbert Guenther, tr., *The Life and Teachings of Nāropa* (London: Oxford University Press, 1963), Nalanda Translation Committee, trs., *The Life of Marpa the Translator* (Boulder: Prajna Press, 1982), and Lobsang P. Lhalungpa, tr., *The Life of Milarepa* (New York: E.P. Dutton, 1977).

39. Dowman, p. 86.

40. *Ibid.*, p. 89.

41. The list "aggression, ignorance, clinging, pride or jealousy" actually enumerates the five root-*kleśa-s* or defilements in Vajrayāna Buddhism. They transmute into the Five Wisdoms of the Five Buddha families. See Chogyam Trungpa, *Cutting Through Spiritual Materialism* (Berkeley: Shambhala, 1973), pp. 217-234.

42. Diana Paul, *Women in Buddhism: Images of the Feminine in Mahāyāna Tradition* (Berkeley: Asian Humanities Press, 1979; Berkeley: University of California Press, 1985). Though much Mahāyāna literature contains highly positive images of women, one also finds quite negative images. The texts here are well arranged and explained so that one can readily see the various strands of Mahāyāna attitudes toward women.

43. Succinct statements of this thesis in feminist theory can

be found in Charlene Spretnek, ed., *The Politics of Women's Spirituality: Essays on the Rise of Spiritual Power Within the Feminist Movement* (New York: Anchor Books, 1982), pp. 510-28 and 565-73.

44. The methodology condensed into this statement is more completely explained in Rita Gross' "Women's Studies in Religion: The State of the Art, 1980," in *Traditions in Contact and Change*, eds. Peter Slater and Donald Wiebe (Waterloo, Ontario, Canada: Wilfrid Laurier Press, 1983), pp. 579-591.

45. This terminology pervades Mary Daly's *Gyn/Ecology: The Metaethics of Radical Feminism* (Boston: Beacon Press, 1978). See especially pp. 252-255 and p. 360. For a review of this position from the Buddhist point of view, see Rita Gross, "Bitterness and Effectiveness: Reflections on Mary Daly's *Gyn/Ecology*," in *Anima: An Experiential Journal*, vol. 7, no. 1 (Fall 1980): pp. 47-51.

46. This use of the term "enlightened society" is a cryptic but direct reference to the tradition of Shambhala, the once and future enlightened society of Tibetan tradition. For some Buddhists, this tradition is completely alive and significant. See Chogyam Trungpa, *Shambhala: The Sacred Path of the Warrior* (Boulder: Shambhala, 1984).

47. Though not yet, to my knowledge, systematically studied, it is commonly noted that new or "frontier" situations tend to allow women greater equality and freedom than is later found in the same situation. This thesis could easily be documented for the origins of Buddhism, Christianity and Islam. But it is also noticeable in many reform movements within religious traditions and even in secular situations. For example, in many Western states, women could vote before women's suffrage forced its allowance thoughout the U.S.

48. Though few people are yet working on this topic, some beginnings have been made. See Rita Gross' "Buddhism and Feminism: Toward Their Mutual Transformation," in *Eastern Buddhist*, vol. 19, nos. 1 and 2 (Spring and Fall 1986).

CHAPTER TWO: DOWN WITH THE DEMONESS

1. "*gDug pa can gyi yul.*" *lHa 'dre bka' thang*, Potala ed., f.21b. Cited by Erik Haarh, *The Yar-luṅ Dynasty* (Kobenhavn: G.E.C. Gad's Forlag, 1969), p. 237. Also Anne-Marie Blondeau, "Le Lha 'dre bKa' than," in *Études Tibétaines dédiées à la mémoire de Marcelle Lalou* (Paris: Adrien Maisonneuve, 1971), p. 73

2. "*Sha za gdong dmar kyi yul.*" *rGyal po'i bka' thang*, as quoted in the introduction to the sNar-thang bKa'-'gyur, index volume, f.14a. Translated by F. W. Thomas, *Tibetan Literary Texts and Documents Concerning Chinese Turkestan* (London: The Royal Asiatic Society, 1935), vol. II, p. 288.

3. "*Yi dwags preta puri bod kyi yul.*" *lHa 'dre bka' thang*, f. 21b.

4. *bTsun mo bka'i thang*, dGa-ldan Phun-tshogs Gling edn., f. 118. Cited by Haarh, p. 322. See also *rGyal rabs bon gyi 'byung gnas*, ed. S. C. Das (Calcutta, 1915), p. 15 cited by R. A. Stein, *Tibetan Civilization*, tr. J. E. Stapleton Driver (Stanford: Stanford University Press, 1972), p. 41.

5. *lHa 'dre bka' thang*, sDe-dge edn., f.4b. Cited by Stein, p. 40.

6. David Snellgrove and Hugh Richardson, *A Cultural History of Tibet* (London: Weidenfeld and Nicolson, 1968), pp. 29-30. Restated from Paul Pelliot, *Histoire ancienne du Tibet* (Paris, 1969), pp. 1-3 and 79-82.

7. William Woodville Rockhill, *The Land of the Lamas* (London: Longnans, Green, and Co., 1891), p. 335 seq.

8. See Giuseppi Tucci, *Preliminary Report on Two Scientific Expeditions in Nepal* (Roma: Istituto Italiano per il Media Ed Estremo Oriente, 1956), p. 92 seq; Rockhill, pp. 339-341; F. W. Thomas, *Ancient Folk-Literature from North-Eastern Tibet* (Berlin: Akademie-verlag Abhandlungen Der Deutschen Akademie Der Wissenschaften Zu Berlin, 1957), part two, p. 103 seq.; and Stein, *Tibetan Civilization*, p. 35.

9. Rockhill, p. 341. (from the *T'ang shu*).

10. Haarh, p. 221 seq.

11. Thomas, *Ancient Folk-Literature*, part two, p. 110. The rest of the text is more generous in tone.

12. Snellgrove and Richardson, p. 58.

13. As in the *Vimalaprabhāparipṛcchā*, tr. Thomas, *Tibetan Literary Texts*, vol. I, p. 221, n. 4. For reflections on the meaning of the word *srin*, see R. A. Stein, "Un ensemble sémantique tibétain: creér et procreér, être et devenir, vivre, nourrir et guerir," *Bulletin of the School of African and Oriental Studies*, vol. 36 (1973): pp. 412-23.

14. E.g. in the *rGyal po bka' thang*, Potala edn., f.18a, cited by Haarh, p. 291. In the *bShad mdzod yid bzhin nor bu*, the *Srin* are the second of eight rulers of Tibet prior to gNya' khri btsan po: See Haarh, p. 294. Brag-srin appears in *La dwags rgyal rabs*: See A. H. Franck, *Antiquities of Indian Tibet* part two (Calcutta: Archeological Survey of India, 1925), pp. 20-21. Many other examples could be given.

15. Tibet as a whole is a *Srin*, as in the *gZer myig*, where gShen rab arrives in "The land of Tibet, the flesh-eating red-faced Srin-po." *bKa' 'dus pa rin po che'i rgyud gzer myig*, f.72a, cited in Haarh, p. 236. Examples of *Srin* connected to particular parts of Tibet are the *Nyang-srin*, *rKong-srin* and *Dags-srin*, from the same passage in the *gZer myig*. The *Byang-srin* and *Kong-srin* are killed by gNya' khri btsan po in the *bShad mdzod yid bzhin nor bu*, cited by Haarh, p. 215. F. W. Thomas also characterizes the *Srin* as being attached to particular areas: *Ancient Folk-Literature*, p. 58. A Red *Srin-mo* of the Earth appears in *Brag btsan mchod bskang*, MS cited by René de Nebesky-Wojkowitz, *Oracles and Demons of Tibet* (London: Oxford University Press and 'S-Gravenhage: Mouton & Co., 1956), p. 252.

16. dPa' bo gtsug lag 'phreng ba, *Chos 'byung mkhas pa'i dga' ston*, f.3a, ed. Lokesh Chandra (New Delhi: International Academy of Indian Culture, 1962), Śata Piṭaka Series vol. 9, in four fascicles.

17. Nebesky-Wojkowitz, p. 280, citing *bKa' brgyud kyi mngon par dregs pa'i dbu phyogs*.

18. Thomas, *Ancient Folk Literature*, ch. 4. This text con-

cerns the sKyi Kingdom and recounts violent struggles with the *Srin*. The female *Srin* that appear include Phyag na yed mo (1.222); Pod ldungs sdu khlad kyi pya khyi ma (1.338); and gNag brang ma (1.341).

19. See Gustave Charles Toussaint, *Le dict de Padma* (Paris: E. Leroux, 1933), p. 247.

20. Nebesky-Wojkowitz, p. 32.

21. Nebesky-Wojkowitz, p. 259.

22. Nebesky-Wojkowitz, p. 280.

23. See Michael Aris's masterful study of the supine *Srin-mo* story, and the temples in Bhutan that are connected to it, in *Bhutan: The Early History of a Himalayan Kingdom* (Warminster: Aris & Phillips Ltd., 1979). See pp. 8-12 for a discussion of the *Maṇi bka' 'bum* and the varying versions of its narratives. See also Matthew Kapstein, "Remarks on the Maṇi Bka' 'bum and the Cult of Avalokiteśvara in Tibet," typescript to be published in a volume based on the proceedings of the Second Annual Conference of the North American Tibetological Society held in Berkeley, August 1980, edited by Ron Davidson and Steven Goodman. The portions of the *Maṇi bka' 'bum* that I have translated below are from the Punakha redaction, published in New Delhi by Trayang and Jamyang Samten, 1975. (2 vols).

24. See below, n. 77.

25. See Aris's list, pp. 291-2, n.11.

26. F. 258 (= 129b).

27. See Aris, p. 292, n. 24.

28. *Maṇi bka' 'bum*, f. 259 (= 130a).

29. *Maṇi bka' 'bum*, f. 260 (= 130b).

30. *Maṇi bka' 'bum*, f.260 (= 130b).

31. See Aris, p. 23 seq. for a discussion of the actual location of these sites.

32. *Maṇi bka' 'bum*, f.273 (136a)

33. See entry on the tortoise by Manabu Warda in *Encyclopedia of Religion*, ed. Mircea Eliade et al (New York: Macmillan Publishing Co., 1987), vol. T, p. 97. Aris, p. 19, cites the *bShad mdzod yid bzhin nor bu* by Don dam smra ba'i seng

ge, ed. Lokesh Chandra (New Delhi, 1969), f. 210a, which states that China was subdued by a female tortoise on her back. According to Stein, *Tibetan Civilization*, pp. 209-10, the dismembered demon is often a turtle in Tibetan legend.

34. *Enuma Elish*, tr. Charles Doria and Harris Lenowitz, *Origins: Creation Texts from the Ancient Mediterranean* (Garden City: Anchor Press/Doubleday, 1976), esp. pp. 208-214.

35. See D. C. Sirkar, *The Śākta Pīṭhas* (Delhi: Motilal Banarsidass, 1973).

36. Helmut Hoffman, *Tibet: A Handbook* (Bloomington: Indiana University Press, n.d.), p. 108.

37. *Edda*. Summarized by P. Grappin in *Larousse World Mythology*, ed. Pierre Grimal (London, New York, Sydney and Toronto: Paul Hamlyn, 1971).

38. *Ṛgveda X*, 90. See Adrain Snodgrass, *The Symbolism of the Stupa* (Ithaca: Southeast Asia Program, Cornell University, 1985), p. 45 seq., quoting from the *Śatapatha Brahmaṇa* and elsewhere. Note that unlike the *Srin-mo*, Puruṣa is laid out prone, i.e., face down, in the *vastu puruṣa maṇḍala*, but like her, his head is to the east and his feet are to the west.

39. See Nick Allen, "Quadripartition of Society in Early Tibetan Sources," in *Journal Asiatique*, 1978, fasc. 3 & 4; and A. W. Macdonald, "Creative Dismemberment Among the Tamang and Sherpas of Nepal," in *Tibetan Studies in Honour of Hugh Richardson*, ed. Michael Aris and Aung San Suu Kyi (Warminster: Aris & Phillips Ltd., 1980), pp. 199-208.

40. Géza Uray, "The Four Horns of Tibet according to the Royal Annals," in *Acta Orientalia Hungarica*, vol. 10, no. 1 (1960): pp. 31-57, shows that the division into four horns was preceded by an earlier system of three horns.

41. Aris, p. 17.

42. See Snodgrass, pp. 45-51.

43. Snodgrass, p. 184 seq., citing *Ṛgveda* II,11,5.

44. Stein, *Tibetan Civilization*, p. 203.

45. Or "steady nail" according to Guiseppi Tucci, *The Tombs of the Tibetan Kings* (Roma: Istituto Italiano per il Media Ed Estremo Oriente, 1956), p. 5. See his discussion of the sig-

nificance of pillars on p. 34 seq. On a trip to Tibet in the summer of 1987, I saw the pillar that Tucci describes that is next to the tomb of Khri lde srong btsan. It has been excavated to its base, and a full half of the pillar which was not visible to Tucci (see his fig. 2) is now in view. Illustrative of the theme of the present paper is the fact that the pillar rests at the base on the back of a tortoise sculpted from stone.

46. Stein, *Tibetan Civilization*, p. 203, citing the *sBas yul padma bkod pa'i gnas yig*, f. 27. I also saw this pillar, intact at bSam-yas, in 1987.

47. Mircea Eliade, *The Sacred and The Profane: The Nature of Religion*, tr. Willard R. Trask (San Diego, New York and London: Harcourt, Brace & World, 1959), p. 54 seq. See also Snodgrass, p. 185, n. 118.

48. "The axis mundi and the phallus: some unrecognized East-West Parallels" in *Folklore Studies in the Twentieth Century*, ed. V.J. Newall, 1980. Also "The Ancient Pillar-cult at Prayāga (Allahabad): Its Pre-Aśokan Origins," in *Journal of the Royal Asiatic Society*, no. 2 (1983).

49. M. Soumié, "China: the Struggle for Power," in *Larousse World Mythology*, p. 286. See also John Major, "New Light on the Dark Warrior," *Journal of Chinese Religions*, nos. 13 & 14 (Fall 1985 & 1986), p. 84.

50. Snodgrass, p. 186, citing the *Dainichikyō* as summarized in *Mikkyō Daijiten*, 6 vols. (Kyoto, 1971), p. 974 seq.

51. See Vincent Scully, *The Earth, The Temple and The Gods: Greek Sacred Architecture* (New Haven and London: Yale University Press, 1962), for a landmark study of the relationship of Greek architecture to the perception of the surrounding environment. The myth of Apollo on p. 109, from Homeric Hymn III.

52. *Maṇi bka' 'bum*, f. 265 (= 134a).

53. Aris, p. 19.

54. Luce Irigaray, *Speculum* (Ithaca: Cornell University Press, 1983), p. 134.

55. See Erwin W. Strauss, "The Upright Posture," in *Phenomenological Psychology. The Selected Papers of Erwin M.*

Strauss, tr. in part by Erling Eng (New York: Basic Books Inc., 1966), p. 137 seq.

56. *Maṇi bka' 'bum*, ch. 34.

57. *Women in Buddhism: Images of the Feminine in Mahāyāna Tradition* (Berkeley: Asian Humanities Press, 1979; Berkeley: University of California Press, 1985).

58. This thesis, of course, would require a separate study. It can be safely asserted, however, that the sexual imagery and symbolism in Tantra gives the feminine figure much more attention than she receives in other forms of Buddhism. In the fully developed form of Tibetan Tantric Buddhism, we find statements such as "The basis for realizing enlightenment is a human body. Male or female—there is no great difference. But if she develops the mind bent on wisdom, the woman's body is better."—from the biography of Ye-śes-mtsho-rgyal (revealed by dPa' bo stag sham rdo rje, and attributed to Nam mkha' snying po), translated by Tarthang Tulku, *Mother of Knowledge: The Enlightenment of Ye shes mtsho rgyal* (Berkeley: Dharma Publishing, 1983), p. 102.

59. In the same biography of Ye-śes-mtsho-rgyal, the heroine bemoans her fate: "I am a woman...Because of my inferior birth, everyone attacks me....Because I am a woman it is hard to follow the Dharma." *Mother of Knowledge*, p. 105. See also Rinchen Lhamo, *We Tibetans* (London: Seeley Service Co., 1926; New York: Potala Publications, 1985), p. 130: "A woman must reincarnate as a man before she can attain Buddhahood."

60. Thomas, *Ancient Folk-Literature*, part two, pp. 77-78. The account of the general decline begins "d(a) *yang s(ri)n gyis myi gyon chan kyi rogs byas phas*..."

61. A. H. Francke, "gZer myig: A Book of the Tibetan Bonpos," in *Aisa Major* (Apr.-Oct. 1924), 262. My translation.

62. See James Hillman, *The Dream and the Underworld* (New York: Harper and Row, 1979), p. 35 seq., for a somewhat parallel distinction between "underground," i.e. instinctual nature, and "underworld," a psychic realm.

63. For a summary of such practices see Hoffman, p. 98

and Stein, *Tibetan Civilization*, pp. 200-201. For a typical Buddhist rendition, see *Mother of Knowledge*, ch. 7.

64. For a general discussion of the problem see Stein, *Tibetan Civilization*, p. 230 seq.; Per Kvaerne's entry on Bon in *Encyclopedia of Religion*, vol. 2; and David Snellgrove, *The Nine Ways of Bon: Excerpts from the gZi-brjid* (London: Oxford University Press, 1967), introduction; and Samten G. Karmay, "A General Introduction to the History and Doctrines of the Bon," *Memoires of the Research Department of the Toyo Bunko* 33 (1975), pp. 171-217.

65. Thu'u bkwan Chos kyi nyi ma, *Grub mtha' shel gyi me long*, Varanasi, n.d. Chapter entitled "Bon gyi grub mtha' byung tshul," f.lb.

66. *Ibid*, f.2b.

67. A. H. Francke, *The Story of the Eighteen Heroes (Preface to the Kesar-Saga)* (Calcutta: Asiatic Society of Bengal, 1905), fasc. 1, pp. 5-8.

68. Thomas, *Ancient Folk-Literature*, part two, p. 89 seq. On p. 105, Thomas connects Myang with one of the Lands of the Women. See R. A. Stein's treatment of this text in "Du récit au rituel dans le manuscrits tibétains de Touen-houang" in *Études Tibétaines dédiées à la mémorie de Marcel Lalou* (Paris: Adrien Maisonneuve, 1971), pp. 479-547.

69. Haarh, p. 326; see Hoffman, p. 94 seq., for a discussion of the three realms.

70. As repeated by Stein, *Tibetan Civilization*, p. 243.

71. From Tun-huang MS 250 du fonds Pelliot, tr. Haarh in his Appendix I.

72. So called in a work by the fifth Dalai Lama, according to Haarh, p. 343. In MS 250 she is called 'O de ring mo.

73. Ernst Cassirer, *The Philosophy of Symbolic Forms.* vol. 2: *Mythical Thinking*, tr. Ralph Manheim (New Haven and London: Yale University Press, 1955).

74. But see Samten G. Karmay, "King Tsa/Dza and Vajrayāna," in *Tantric and Taoist Studies in Honour of R. A. Stein*, ed. Michel Strickman, vol. 1 (Bruxelles: Institut Belge des Hautes Etudes Chinoises, 1981), pp. 192-211. In Pelliot tibé-

taine no. 840, this king is portrayed as a supporter of Buddhism.

75. I.e., the Chinese princess, Kong jo, of the *Maṇi bka' 'bum* account cited earlier.

76. = lCags-po-ri.

77. R. A. Stein, *Une Chronique ancienne de dSam yas* (Paris, 1961), pp. 78-79. My translation.

78. "Gangā: The Goddess in Hindu Sacred Geography," in *The Divine Consort*, ed. John Stratton Hawley and Donna Marie Huff (Berkeley: Graduate Theological Union, 1982), p. 182.

79. Nebesky-Wojkowitz, ch. 14.

80. From the *Bon rin po che 'phrul dag bden pa gtsang ma klu 'bum*, summarized by Stein, *Tibetan Civilization*, pp. 244-245.

81. As noted by Aris in *Bum thang dar gud kyi lung bstan* (Aris, p. 291, n.4). See also A. H. Francke, *Antiquities*, p. 152, where in the chronicles of Zangs-dkar, Padmasambhava holds down the *sa-bkra* (= sa-dgra) and builds monasteries on the head, heart and feet of a supine *Srin-mo.*

CHAPTER THREE: AN ECSTATIC SONG

1. James Robinson, tr. *Buddha's Lions: The Lives of the Eighty-Four Siddhas* (Berkeley: Dharma Pub., 1979), pp 250-253; George Roerich, tr. *Blue Annals* (Delhi: Motilal Banarsidass, 1949; rpt. 1976), p. 290; Lama Chimpa and Alaka Chattopadhyaya, tr. *Tāranātha's History of Buddhism in India* (Atlantic Highlands: Humanities Press, 1981), p. 214n; David Templeman, tr. *Seven Instruction Lineages by Jo.nong Tāranātha* (Dharamsala: Library of Tibetan Works and Archives, 1983) p. 36; B. Datta, tr. *Mystic Tales of Lama Tāranātha*, (Calcutta: Ramakrishna Vedanta Math, 1944), p. 21; Benoytosh Bhattacharyya, *Introduction to Buddhist Esotericism* (Delhi : Motilal Banarsidass, 1980), pp. 77-78. Lakṣmīṅkarā's student Jālandharipa is of lowcaste origin, which distinguishes him from the brahmin *mahāsiddha* Jālandharapa.

2. *Sahajasiddhipaddhatināma*, Derge 2261, directly following Indrabhūti's *Sahajasiddhi*; *Vajrayoginīsādhana*, Derge 1547; and *Vajrayānacaturdaśamūlapattivṛtti*, Derge 2485.

3. Derge 2220. A translation of the *Advayasiddhi* has been published by Malati J. Shendge, *M. S. University Oriental Series*, no. 8 (Baroda: Oriental Institute, 1964).

4. See *Advayasiddhi*, verses 4, 5, 21.

5. *Dohās* are sometimes called *caryāpādas* or *caryāgīti*; they also occur in other Indian religious contexts. For general discussions and translations of Buddhist *dohās*, see Per Kvaerne, *An Anthology of Buddhist Tantric Songs*, (Oslo: Universitetsforlaget, 1977); Atindra Mojumder, *Caryāpadas* (Calcutta: Naya Prokash, 1967); and Herbert Guenther, *Royal Song of Saraha* (Berkeley and London: Shambala, [1968] 1973).

6. Derge 2433.

CHAPTER FOUR: ḌĀKINĪ

1. This characterization of *ḍākinī* is found in the "Glossaries" appended to both *The Life of Marpa the Translator* (Boulder: Prajna Press, 1982), p. 219 and *The Rain of Wisdom* (Boulder: Shambhala, 1980), p. 345. Both works were translated by the Nalanda Translation Committee under the direction of Chogyam Trungpa Rinpoche.

2. For example, this gloss is used by Keith Dowman in the title of his translation of the life of the *ḍākinī*, Ye-śes-mtsho-rgyal. See his *Sky Dancer; The Secret Life and Songs of the Lady Yeshe Tsogyel* (London: Routledge & Kegan Paul, 1984).

3. See Geshe Kelsang Gyatso's *Clear Light of Bliss; Mahamudra in Vajrayana Buddhism* (London: Wisdom Publications, 1982).

4. Both "Glossaries" mentioned above in note #1 define *ḍākinī* as "a wrathful or semiwrathful female yidam."

5. A. Waddell often referred to *ḍākinī-s* as being "demoniacal." Waddell, Evans-Wentz, and Das all used the term "witch" in their characterizations.

6. See Waddell, *Tibetan Buddhism* (London: Allen & Co., 1895; New York: Dover Publications, 1972), p. 366.

7. Sarat Chandra Das used both "sprites" and "fairies" in his definition of the term, *mkha' 'gro ma*. See his *A Tibetan-English Dictionary* (rpt., Delhi: Motilal Banarsidass, 1970), p. 180. (Interestingly, "fairies" is also the term used by Robert Paul in his *The Tibetan Symbolic World; Psychoanalytic Explorations* [Chicago: The University of Chicago Press, 1982]. On p. 132, for example, he calls *ḍākinī-s* "sky-going fairies.")

8. This is one of the descriptions used by Anagarika Govinda. See his *Foundations of Tibetan Mysticism* (London: Rider and Company, 1960; New York: Samuel Weiser, Inc., 1975), p. 192.

9. Here I am playing upon the title of Robert Paul's valuable work, of the same name.

10. See Nathan Katz's "Anima and mKha'-'gro-ma: A Critical Comparative Study of Jung and Tibetan Buddhism," in *The Tibet Journal*, vol. 2, no. 3 (Autumn 1977), pp. 13-43.

11. Waddell, *op. cit.*, p. 180.

12. *Ibid.*, p. 129-130.

13. Das, *op. cit.*, p. 180.

14. *Ibid.*, p. 180.

15. See Snellgrove, *Buddhist Himālaya* (Oxford: Bruno Cassirer, 1957), p. 175.

16. Kalff, "Dakinis in the Cakrasaṃvara Tradition," in *Tibetan Studies*, ed. M. Brauen and P. Kvaerne (Zurich: Volkerkundemuseum der Universitat Zurich, 1978), pp. 149-162.

17. *Ibid.*, pp. 149-150.

18. *Ibid.*, p. 150.

19. *Ibid.*, p. 150.

20. For two interesting translations of Padmasambhava's "journey" to Tibet, see Keith Dowman's *The Legend of the Great Stupa and the Life of the Lotus Born Guru* (Berkeley: Dharma Publishing, 1973), pp. 82-85; and *Crystal Mirror IV* (Berkeley: Tibetan Nyingma Meditation Center, 1975), pp. 18-25.

21. See Garma C. C. Chang, *Teachings of Tibetan Yoga* (1963 rpt., Secaucus, N.J.: Citadel Press, 1977), p. 122. (An interest-

ing note on the inadequacy of this definition is provided by John Wilson in his "Introduction" to this work, pp. 8-9.)

22. This suggestion was posited by James Robinson in his translation, *Buddha's Lions; The Lives of the Eighty-Four Siddhas* (Berkeley: Dharma Publishing, 1979), p. 394.

23. The definition of *ḍākinī* as "a female imp attending Kālī (feeding on human flesh)" is found in Sir Monier-Williams' A *Sanskrit-English Dictionary* (1899; rpt. Oxford: Clarendon Press, 1964), p. 430. J. N. Banerjea, in *Paurāṇic and Tāntric Religion* (Calcutta: University of Calcutta, 1966), p. 128, states that "the later lexicons explain the name Ḍākinī as a special kind of the attendants of Kālī (*Ḍākinī Kālīgaṇaviśeshaḥ*)" and suggests that an earlier or parallel phenomenon may have been the *ghoshiṇī* who occur in the *Atharvaveda* as the "female attendants of the terrific god Rudra."

24. See Guenther, *Treasures on the Tibetan Middle Way* (Berkeley: Shambhala, 1971), p. 103, n. 1. Cf. Katz, op. cit., p. 24.

25. Govinda, *op. cit.*, p. 196.

26. Robinson, *op. cit.*, p. 394.

27. Wittgenstein, *Philosophical Investigations,* tr. G. E. M. Anscombe (Oxford: Basil Blackwell 1958). The fuller statement by Wittgenstein, found in P.I., p. 43, is: "For a *large* class of cases—though not for all—in which we employ the word 'meaning' it can be explained thus: the meaning of a word is its use in the language." Wittgenstein was aware of two other points of importance to this study; namely, he realized that language has *multiple* functions, and that words and expressions function *relationally*, getting their meanings in social [and/or cultural] contexts.

28. This language is that used by Lobsang Lhalungpa in the "Introduction" to his translation of *The Life of Milarepa* (New York: E.P. Dutton, 1977), p. xxiii.

29. See Guenther's translation, *The Life and Teaching of Nāropa* (Oxford: Oxford University Press, 1963; rpt. 1974), pp. 24-25.

30. Guenther, *Treasures on the Tibetan Middle Way*, p. 103, n. 1. Also cited in Katz, op. cit., p. 13.

31. Guenther clearly recognizes the parallels between the *ḍākinī* and Jung's *anima*. In a note to this passage, he writes: "This aspect has a great similarity to what the Swiss psychologist C. G. Jung calls the 'anima.' " Katz's article, *op. cit.*, investigates and elaborates upon these similarities; and upon some dissimilarities.

32. Bhupendranath Datta, tr. *Mystic Tales of Lāmā Tārānātha* (Calcutta: Ramakrishna Vedanta Math, 1944; rpt. 1957), p. 65. This story, with some minor changes in translation, is also cited in Katz, *op. cit.*, p. 23. It is paraphrased in Tsultrim Allione's *Women of Wisdom* (London: Routledge & Kegan Paul, 1984), p. 37.

33. This type of language was used, one may recall, in several of Carlos Castaneda's novels for describing part of the method, and experience, of training in the Yaqui Indian tradition. See especially Castaneda's *Journey to Ixtlan; The Lessons of Don Juan* (New York: Simon and Schuster, 1972).

34. Katz, *op. cit.*, p. 22. (I have slightly rearranged the structure of Katz's original sentence here.)

35. These remarks by Chogyam Trungpa Rinpoche are to be found in the journal *Maitreya IV*, p. 25. They are also quoted in Allione, op. cit., p. 38.

36. This *rnam thar* and that of Saṅs-rgyas-ye-śes (which follows) were translated by me. The complete translations of these *rnam thar*, together with four others, will shortly appear in a book forthcoming from Wisdom Publications entitled *Enlightened Beings; Early dGe-lugs Siddha Biographies.*

37. See Katz, *op. cit.*, p. 27.

38. For the story of Kukkuripa, see Robinson's *Buddha's Lions*, pp. 128-130; and Keith Dowman's *Masters of Mahāmudrā* (Albany: SUNY Press, 1985), pp. 199-203.

39. Often the term *karmamudrā* is used in such contexts as an alternative for *rig ma*. However, in my opinion, there is already so much confusion regarding the many, and varied, meanings of *karmamudrā* that I prefer not to use it.

40. An interesting analysis of the benefits of having an actual flesh and blood partner, and of "living with an insightful

consort" is presented in Allione, *op. cit.*, pp. 39-40.

41. Katz, *op. cit.*, p. 24.

42. *Ibid.*, p. 24.

43. There is as yet no full-scale biography of Ni-gu-ma published in English. One can, however, learn something of her life from Guenther's translation of *The Life and Teaching of Nāropa*. Additional information can be gleaned from *The Blue Annals*, tr. Roerich (1949; rpt. Delhi: Motilal Banarsidass, 1979); and from Glenn Mullin's *Selected Works of the Dalai Lama II* (Ithaca, N.Y.: Snow Lion Publications, 1985).

44. There are two English translations of the life of Ye-śes-mtsho-rgyal: 1) Tarthang Tulku's translation, called *Mother of Knowledge; the Enlightenment of Ye-shes mTsho-rgyal* (Berkeley: Dharma Publishing, 1983); and 2) Keith Dowman's *Sky Dancer; The Secret Life and Songs of the Lady Yeshe Tsogyel* (London: Routledge & Kegan Paul, 1984).

45. Again, there is no single work which narrates the life of bDag-med-ma, but information regarding her may be gleaned from *The Blue Annals* and from *The Life of Marpa the Translator.*

46. Apart from the accounts of it in *The Blue Annals*, the life of Ma-gcig-lab-sgron-ma appears in Allione's *Women of Wisdom*, pp. 141-187. Additionally, four of the "Eighty-four siddhas" of Indian fame were women. Their life stories can be found in Robinson's *Buddha's Lions* and in Keith Dowman's *Masters of Mahāmudrā*.

47. Katz, *op. cit.*, p. 28. In the quote, I have substituted "siddha" for Katz's phonetic rendering of its Tibetan equivalent.

48. *Ibid.*, p. 28.

49. In essence these "two" goddesses are actually one. Vajrayoginī is the female deity who is the chief consort of Lord Cakrasaṃvara. It is explained that the name "Vajravārāhī" (that is, "Diamond Sow") is used of her to emphasize her *function* (which is to destroy the ignorance of holding the view of an inherently existent "I"—symbolized by the pig's head), while the name "Vajrayoginī" is used to indicate her *essence* (namely,

the adamantine insight which cognizes the inseparability of bliss and voidness.)

50. Here, I describe Vajrayoginī's iconographic form based upon the descriptions of it found in a number of her meditative *sādhanas*. For a description and discussion of the iconographic form of Vajravārāhī and her "ornaments," see Allione, *op. cit.*, pp. 31-36.

51. That is, the *Vajracchedikā-sūtra*, one of the group of smaller *sūtra-s* comprising the "Prajñāpāramitā," or "Transcendent Wisdom," literature.

52. From Edward Conze's translation of the *Vajracchedikā*. See his *Buddhist Wisdom Books* (London: George Allen & Unwin, Ltd., 1958; rpt. 1980), p. 63. For Conze's "Dharma-bodies" I have substituted "Dharmakāya."

53. This translation is quoted from Robert A. F. Thurman's *The Holy Teaching of Vimalakīrti; A Mahāyāna Scripture* (University Park: The Pennsylvania State University Press, 1976), p. 61.

54. For a full enumeration and discussion of these, see my *The Diamond Light of the Eastern Dawn* (New York: Simon and Schuster, 1972), pp. 100-106.

55. It is, I believe too simplistic to assert that the Tantras are written from a male point of view because most tantric practitioners were/are men. I would agree that the texts do seem to take this point of view. However, there seem in addition actually to be qualities that are "feminine" in nature, and that hence require feminine characterization. A thorough discussion of such a premise would, of course, require at least a book.

56. I find this way of speaking more appropriate, and much more helpful, than language like: the *ḍākinī* represents one's "other" or one's "opposite." It seems to me to be also less combative; and certainly, if we're seeking Enlightenment, we had better try to be less combative.

57. For explanations and descriptions of the *ḍākinī* based upon this three-fold schema of outer, inner, and secret, I am grateful to Geshe Jampel Thar-'dod.

CHAPTER FIVE: MOVING TOWARD A SOCIOLOGY OF TIBET

1. *Myths of Male Dominance* (New York: Monthly Review Press, 1981), p. 134.

2. Anne C. Klein, "Primordial Purity and Everyday Life: Exalted Female Symbols and the Women of Tibet," in *Immaculate and Powerful: The Female in Sacred Image and Reality*, ed. C. W. Atkinson, C. H. Buchanan and M. R. Miles (Boston: Beacon Press, The Harvard Women's Studies in Religion Series, 1985).

3. B. N. Aziz, "Women in Tibetan Society and Tibetology," paper presented at the International Tibetan Studies Seminar, 1985, at Munich, presently in press, edited by H. Uebach.

4. Klein, p. 132.

5. Janice D. Willis, "Tibetan *Ani-s:* The Nun's Life in Tibet" in this volume. This article originally appeared in *The Tibet Journal*, vol. 4, no. 4, pp. 14-32.

6. *Studies in the History of Buddhism*, ed. A. K. Narain (Delhi: B.R. Publishing, 1980), pp. 155-166.

7. Aziz, *op. cit.*

8. *Ibid.* and B. N. Aziz, *Tibetan Frontier Families* (New Delhi: Vikas Publishing Co., 1978).

9. Edwin Bernbaum in his *The Way to Shambhala* (New York: Anchor Doubleday, 1980) sought out no women in his interviews with Shambhala-goers.

10. *Women in Buddhism: Images of the Feminine in Mahāyāna Tradition*, 2nd ed. (Berkeley: University of California Press, 1985).

11. Wendy O'Flaherty, *Asceticism and Eroticism in the Mythology of Shiva* (London: Oxford University Press, 1973) and *The Origins of Evil in Hindu Mythology* (Berkeley: University of California Press, 1976).

12. *Dangerous Wives and Sacred Sisters* (New York: Columbia University Press, 1983).

13. See D. Jacobsen, "Golden Handprints and Red-Painted Feet: Hindu Childbirth Rituals in Central India" and Susan

S. Wadley, "Hindu Women's Family and Household Rites in a North Indian Village" in *Unspoken Worlds*, ed. N A. Falk and R. M. Gross (San Francisco: Harper and Row, 1980).

14. "Laksminkara, a Woman *siddha*," *LOKA 2, Journal of the Nāropa Institute* (New York: Anchor Doubleday, 1976), pp. 36-42 and "Accomplished Women in Tantric Buddhism of Medieval India and Tibet," in *Unspoken Worlds*, ed. Falk and Gross.

15. *The Tibetan Symbolic World, Psychoanalytic Interpretations* (Chicago: University of Chicago Press, 1982).

16. Rinchen D. Taring, *Daughter of Tibet* (Delhi: Allied Publishers, 1970) and Tseten Dolkar, *Girl from Tibet* (Chicago: Loyola University Press, 1971).

17. *Women of Wisdom* (London: Routledge & Kegan Paul, 1984).

18. James F. Fisher, *Trans-Himalayan Traders; Economy, Society and Culture in Northwest Nepal* (Berkeley: University of California Press, 1980), pp. 75-79.

19. E. Leacock and H. Safa, *Women's Work: Development and the Division of Labor by Gender* (New York: Bergen and Garvey, 1986).

20. P. Kaplanian, "Quelques Aspects du Mythe et Des Structures Mentales au Ladakh," in *Recent Research on Ladakh*, ed. R. Kantowsky and R. Sander (Munchen: Weltforum Verlag, 1983).

21. Kathryn March, "Weaving, Writing and Gender," *Man* n.s. 18, pp. 729-744.

22. Kaplanian, pp. 93-106.

23. March, p. 729.

CHAPTER SIX: TIBETAN *ANI-S*

1. This English translation by Tarthang Tulku is found in *Mother of Knowledge: The Enlightenment of Ye-shes mTsho-rgyal* (Berkeley: Dharma Publishing, 1985), p. 105.

2. That Padmasambhava was not alone in this important en-

deavor has been amply shown by recent scholarship. See for example Eva Dargyay's study, *The Rise of Esoteric Buddhism in Tibet*, (Delhi: Motilal Banarsidass, 1977) which goes a long way towards filling-out the actual historical circumstances and figures involved in the early establishment of Buddhism in Tibet. Dr. Dargyay shows that such figures as Vimalamitra and Vairocana were of equal (or even more) importance to the founding of the earliest, i.e., rNying-ma, tradition there.

3. Two recent translations of Ye-śes-mtsho-rgyal's *rnam thar* have been published: 1) Tarthang Tulku's *Mother of Knowledge* and 2) Keith Dowman's *Sky Dancer: the Secret Life and Songs of the Lady Yeshe Tsogyel* (London: Routledge & Kegan Paul, 1984).

4. English translation given in *Mother of Knowledge*, p. 102.

5. As examples, see Nancy Falk and Rita Gross, eds., *Unspoken Worlds: Women's Religious Lives in Non-Western Cultures* (San Francisco: Harper & Row, 1979); and Judith Plaskow and Joan Arnold, eds., *Women and Religion* (Chico, CA: AAR/Scholars Press, 1974).

6. See, for example, Nancy Falk, "An Image of Woman in Old Buddhist Literature: the Daughters of Māra," in *Women and Religion* pp. 102-12; Diana Paul, *Women in Buddhism; Images of the Feminine in the Mahāyāna Tradition* (Berkeley: Asian Humanities Press, 1979; reprinted in paperback by the University of California Press, Berkeley, 1985); Nancy Schuster, "Changing the Female Body: Wise Women and the Bodhisattva Career in Some *Mahāratnakūṭasūtras*," in *The Journal of the International Association of Buddhist Studies*, vol. 4, no. 1 (1981):24-69; André Bareau, "Un Personnage Bien Mysterieux: L'espouse du Buddha," in *Indological and Buddhist Studies; Volume in Honour of Professor J. W. deJong* (Canberra: Faculty of Asian Studies, 1982), pp. 31-59; and Yuichi Kajiyama, "Women in Buddhism," in *Eastern Buddhist*, n.s. 15, no. 2 (Autumn 1982): 53-70.

7. I have argued this point somewhat differently and more fully in an article entitled "Nuns and Benefactresses: the Role of Women in the Development of Buddhism" in *Women, Re-*

ligion and Social Change, Y. Haddad and E. Findly, eds. (Albany: SUNY Press, 1985), pp. 59-85.

8. To date, only the life of Ye-śes-mtsho-rgyal has received full treatment in English translation. Abbreviated biographies of the four female luminaries of the famed Indian "eighty-four siddha(s)" appear in James Robinson's *Buddha's Lions; the Lives of the Eighty-Four Siddhas* (Berkeley: Dharma Press, 1979) and in Keith Dowman's *Masters of Mahāmudrā* (Albany, N.Y: SUNY Press, 1985); and brief accounts of some of the eminent female followers of Pha Dam-pa Saṅs-rgyas (called "nuns" (*Tib. ma-jo*) or "ladies" (*jo-mo*)) are given in *The Blue Annals* tr. George Roerich (1949 rpt. Delhi: Motilal Banarsidass, 1979), pp. 915-920. However, full treatment of such female tantric adepts as Ni-gu-ma, Ma-gcig-lab-sgron-ma, and bDag-med-ma remain to be done. Several American women are presently working on translations of the lives of these women.

9. I use the term (*chos-pa*) here in its technical, rather than general sense. Generally, in Tibetan, *chos-pa* refers to any follower of the Buddha's Dharma (Tib. *chos*). Here, however, it is used specifically in reference to a practitioner who has some training in particular disciplines/ritual.

10. For more information on *lha-kha-s* and *dpa'-mo-s*, see Barbara Aziz, *Tibetan Frontier Families* (New Delhi: Vikas Publishing House, 1978), es. p. 253; and Per-Arne Berglie, "On the Question of Tibetan Shamanism," in *Tibetan Studies* (Zurich: Völkerkundermuseum der Universität Zürich, 1978), pp. 39-51.

11. See n. 8 above.

12. For recent accounts of the nuns' tradition in India and Śri Lanka, see Nancy Falk, "The Case of the Vanishing Nuns: the Fruits of Ambivalence in Ancient Indian Buddhism," in *Unspoken Worlds; Women's Religious Lives in Non-Western Cultures*, pp. 207-224; and Ellen Goldberg, "Buddhist nuns make comeback in Sri Lanka—to monks' dislike," in *The Christian Science Monitor*, April 2, 1984, p. 14 and 44.

13. Tsepon W. D. Shakabpa. *Tibet; A Political History* (New

Haven: Yale University Press, 1967). Shakabpa's population figures are given on p. 6.

14. I suspect that both these figures are considerably higher than the actual number of monks and nuns in pre-1959 Tibet.

15. *Op. cit.*, pp. 6-7.

16. The distortions introduced by translating the term *dgon-pa* in English as "monastery" have not gone unnoticed by David Snellgrove. See for example his discussion in *Buddhist Himālaya* (Oxford: Bruno Cassirer, 1957), pp. 200-201.

The proper translation and application of the Tibetan term also may be seen to explain how it is that each of the four major Tibetan Buddhist traditions, now in exile, commonly estimates the number of *dgon-pa* belonging to each of their respective sects as 2,000-3,000 establishments. For example, Tarthang Tulku, a teacher of the *rNying-ma* tradition, in *Crystal Mirror V*, (a publication put out in 1977), estimates that there were in Tibet 3,000 rNying-ma *dgon-pa*. He provides a listing of such establishments together with the enrollments at each. A few were relatively large complexes with upwards of 1,000 members. Most had populations of under one hundred, and some are listed which had only *one* member.

17. Of course, this non-specificity with regard to the sex of a member of a given religious community is also echoed in the original meaning of the English term "convent." The term derives from the Latin *conventus* i.e., "a coming together; an assembly." Only later did the term come to be popularly applied specifically to a place where nuns convened.

18. David Snellgrove, *A Cultural History of Tibet* (1968; rpt. Boulder: Prajna Press, 1980), pp. 247-248.

19. Barbara Aziz, *Tibetan Frontier Families*, p. 228.

20. The chief cause of hardships for Buddhist nuns, of whatever country or historical period, was economic. Tibet was no exception here. But, as I and some others (Diana Paul and Nancy Falk for example) have argued, the nuns' troubles were also created by an ambivalent image, fostered by some Buddhist literature, of women's ability to successfully practice the renunciant's life.

One other feature peculiar to Tibetan monastic life should be mentioned here, namely, the so-called "monk-/nun-tax, or levy." C. W. Cassinelli and Robert Ekvall, in *A Tibetan Principality; the Political System of Sa-skya* (Ithaca: Cornell University Press, 1969), explore the workings of this system of conscripting monks and nuns in Sa-skya. For monks, their study shows, this system often proved to be of benefit, offering upward mobility. The same was not so for the nuns. In two dramatically different descriptions, Cassinelli and Ekvall report on page 296, of monks:

> "Levy monks had certain advantages over volunteer monks, especially the opportunity for attaining personal wealth. This opportunity—and the general advantages of monkhood, such as education, high prestige, material comfort, proximity to the sources of power and authority, and the chance to become a sKu Drag official—apparently made the levy of monks a quite bearable institution. Moreover, the family that produced a boy upon call had its revenue lowered in compensation. It must also be remembered that the average Tibetan family felt a kind of duty to provide at least one son to the monkhood."

And on p. 297, of nuns:

> "There was also a levy of nuns to staff the two nunneries near the capital, Sa bZang and Rin Chen sGang, with a total of about 110 nuns, of whom not more than 10 per cent were volunteers. The nun levy was also based on the schedule of revenue in kind, and a family that gave up a little girl also had its revenue lowered. The levy of nuns, like the levy of monks, no doubt helped tie the polity together, but in a much less significant way. The life of a nun had few attractions. Monks always served as abbots of the nunneries and hence only lesser positions were open to the nuns. No nuns were sent out of Sa sKya proper, and the most a nun could aspire to was becoming a personal servant of the royal family, usually of its unmarried daugh-

ters. Ordinary nuns, moreover, usually had to spend about half their time in physical labor outside their nunneries. The levy of nuns was probably the only way to keep enough nuns in the capital nunneries in order to maintain the religious prestige of the sect."

21. Except for a fairly early Indian anthology of nuns' "triumphant songs" (or *añña-s*) known as the *Therīgāthā* (which is also our main source for claiming an early tradition of women *arhat-s* (those who have attained Nirvāṇa) and of famed women teachers) nuns do not appear in the later literature. In India, Gautama Buddha (563-483 B.C.) had been reluctant to establish an order of nuns and though he had finally agreed to do so, his enjoining of the so-called eight "weighty regulations" (*Pāli: garudhamma*) upon the female order had fixed forever its inferior status vis-à-vis the monkhood.

In *Women in Buddhism*, p. 82, Diana Paul notes:

"...the nun's life is not well marked in the Mahāyāna sutra tradition or in the philosophical writing of that tradition. Participation in an intellectual life by the Mahāyāna Buddhist nun is not recorded. The nun seems not to have been a significant part of the student body of the great Buddhist universities which were the central gem in the crown of the monk's order, an order which was extensive, prosperous, and productive of extraordinary thought and art."

And Nancy Falk writes in "The Case of the Vanishing Nuns," p. 208:

"At the root, the major problem of the women's order probably rested in the Buddhist tradition's inability to affirm completely the idea of women pursuing the renunciant's role. This led to an institutional structure that offered women admirable opportunities for spiritual and intellectual growth, but not for the institutional and scholarly leadership that such growth should have fitted them to assume. The nuns' troubles were compounded by an ambivalent image created in a tradition of Buddhist stories that sometimes praised their achievements but just as often undercut and attacked them."

22. L. Austine Waddell, *Tibetan Buddhism* (1895; rpt. New York: Dover Publications, 1972), p. 275.

23. *Ibid.*, p. 275.

24. Giuseppe Tucci, *To Lhasa and Beyond; Diary of the Expedition to Tibet in the year MCMXLVIII* (Rome: Instituto Poligrafico Dell Stato, 1956), p. 64.

25. See Turrell Wylie's translation, *The Geography of Tibet According to the 'Dzam-gling-rgyas-bshad* (Rome: Is. M.E.O., 1962), pp. 73-74, 144, and 271.

26. Rinchen Dolma Taring, *Daughter of Tibet* (1970; rpt. New Delhi: Allied Publishers, 1978), p. 167.

27. Waddell, *op. cit.*, p. 276.

28. Taring, *op. cit.*, p. 167.

29. *Ibid.*, p. 167.

30. The current incarnation, aged 50, occupies a government office in the Chinese-controlled Tibetan Autonomous Region.

31. Ma-gcig-lab-sgron-ma, famed in Tibetan religious annals as the fashioner of the *gCod* system of tantric practice, is said, in turn, to have been the reincarnation of Ye-śes-mtsho-rgyal.

32. Taring, *op. cit.*, p. 165.

33. *Ibid.*, page facing p. 225.

34. Lobsang Lhalungpa, the son of a powerful ex-State Oracle of Tibet, has written many important works dealing with Tibetan Buddhism, not least of which is his fine English translation of *The Life of Milarepa* (New York: E. P. Dutton, 1977).

35. See *Parabola*, vol. 3, no. 4 (November 1978): p. 49.

36. I join with many others in mourning the recent passing of both these revered teachers of the dGe-lugs tradition.

37. See *Tibet—the Sacred Realm: Photographs 1880-1950* (New York: Aperture, 1983), p. 33. Lhalungpa continues his description of Ani Lochen with the following:

> Endorsing my eclectic attitude, she said to me: "I always looked upon every Buddhist order as being a

different vehicle capable of transporting fortunate seekers across the great ocean of Saṃsāra [the cycle of birth and death].'' The essence of her message can be summed up as follows: What matters most in this troubled world is compassion and wisdom. The form and institution of the practice matters less. A seeker who perceives the illusory nature of all things is on the threshold of wisdom.

38. Taring, *op. cit.*, p. 269.

39. Barbara Aziz, *Tibetan Frontier Families*, p. 244. Aziz first published materials regarding this *ani* in an article entitled ''Ani Chodon: Portrait of a Buddhist Nun,'' in *Loka 2, Journal of the Nāropa Institute* (New York: Doubleday/Anchor) 1976.

40. Aziz, *Tibetan Frontier Families*, p. 244.

41. *Ibid.*, p. 245.

42. *Ibid.*, pp. 245-246.

43. For more on this particular monastery in Kyi-rong (sKyid-grong), see Turrell Wylie, tr., *The Geography of Tibet*, pp. 65 and 129. Wylie notes, p. 129, that ''this monastery is reported as having been erected at the place where Ras-pa zhi-ba-'od, a disciple of Milarepa, had meditated. Later on, it was changed into a Dge-lugs-pa monastery by Kong-po Chab-nag-pa Sangs-rgyas-dpal-'byor, a lama of the Shel-dkar Chos-sde monastery. He established a new school there and gave it this name.'' (I am currently preparing a fuller study of this monastery which supports a different provenance of it.)

44. It is to be noted here that Ani Dol-kar did not at first equate ''freedom'' with the lack of material hardship; rather she spoke of it in political terms. Still, as her subsequent comments reveal, the realities of economic and material hardship and nonfreedom once again enter into her description.

45. These nuns apparently had all been formerly associated with the bSam-gtan-gling dgon-pa.

46. Aziz, *op. cit.*, p. 245.

47. *Ibid.*, p. 243.

CHAPTER SEVEN: TIBETAN NUNS AND NUNNERIES

1. The nunneries listed below were shown to have housed more than one hundred nuns each:

	Name	*Tradition*	*Location*	*Number of Nuns*
1.	dGe-chak Thek-chen-gling	bKa'-brgyud	Nang-chen	1000
2.	sByor-dge sGrol-ri Zhabs-gYon bTzun-dgon	dGe-lugs	Brag-gyab	600
3.	sNgaks-khung-dgon	"	rTa'u-khul	500
4.	Dil-lho-dgon	rNying-ma	sDe-dge-khul	450
5.	A-gro-dgon	dGe-lugs	Tre-hor-'go	300
6.	Ngor-dgon	rNying-ma	Tre-hor-jo-khul	300
7.	Ya-nga gZam-mda'-dgon	dGe-lugs	rGyal-sTon-khul	300
8.	bSam-gTan-gling	"	Ra-sgreng-dgon-wa'i-shar-ngo	200
9.	Bo-ra bTzun-dgon	rNying-ma	gZyi-ka-nyuk	200
10.	A-dkar-yang-dgon	"	Go-jo-mngas-khul	200
11.	Shes-lad-dgon	"	sDe-dge-khul	200
12.	sBe-rgen-dgon	bKa'-brgyud	Tre-hor-dar-rgyas	200
13.	rTa'u-bTzun-dgon	dGe-lugs	rTa'u-khul	200
14.	Dar-cha-ri'i bTzun-dgon	"	Nag-chu-khul	160
15.	Shugs-sems-dgon	rNying-ma	sNe'u-gzhis-khongs-snye-phu	150
16.	Padma Chos-sding-dgon	dGe-lugs	bZhang-mthong-mon	150
17.	Ras-lung-dgon	bKa'-brgyud	rGyal-rtze-khul	150
18.	bTzun-ma-dgon	dGe-lugs	Kong-rag	150
19.	rTze-ri-dgon	rNying-ma	'Ba'-khul	150
20.	Chos-'khor-gling	bKa'-brgyud	Re-che-khul	150
21.	sBa-khug-dgon	rNying-ma	rMar-Khams	130
22.	Brag-dkar Chos-skar	dGe-lugs	Tre-hor-dkar-mdzes	130
23.	Lo-lan-phea-ma-bug	bKa'-brgyud	rGya-mtso-khul	120
24.	Kho-mar-yar-khrod Ri-khrod	dGe-lugs	Brag-gyab	110
25.	'Bum-ri-khrod	rNying-ma	Li-thang	110
26.	Gu-ru Choes-lung-dgon	bKa'-brgyud	Re-che-khul	110

27. Ne-chung-ri-dgon	dGe-lugs	Se-ra'i-shar-ngos-ri-steng	100
28. Rin-sding-dgon	"	Phan-bo-mkhar-rtze-khul	100
29. Pa-tsab-lo-tza'-dgon	"	Phan-bo-za-lha-gzhis-og	100
30. Brag-skyes-dgon	"	gZhis-ka-rtze-khul	100
31. Thos-bsam-gling	"	Shel-dkar-khul	100
32. Be'u-hor-gos-dgon	bKa'-brgyud	sNye-smon	100
33. Chu-bzang-dgon	"	"	100
34. Byams-gling bTzun-dgon	rNying-ma	gLing-khul	100
35. Gru-gu gSer-sde-dgon	"	Chab-mdo	100
36. mKho-mo-dge'-phel Ri-khrod	dGe-lugs	Brag-gyab	100
37. Ra-chu-kha-mdok Nyag-bla-dgon	rNying-ma	Go-co-mngas-khul	100
38. Zangs-ra bTzun-dgon	dGe-lugs	Tre-hor-brag-'go	100
39. Ha-'du bTzun-dgon	"	Tre-hor-dar-rgyas	100
40. Rin-chen-sgang	bKa'-brgyud	Re-che-khul	100
41. mKha'-gling bTzun-dgon	dGe-lugs	lHo-rdzong-khul	100

2. George N. Roerich, tr., *The Blue Annals*, (Delhi: Motilal Banarsidass, 1976), p. 1044.

3. *Ibid.*, pp. 915-20.

4. Janice D. Willis, "Tibetan *Ani-s*; The Nun's Life in Tibet", *The Tibet Journal*, vol. IX, no. 4, 1984: pp. 20-23. (This essay is reprinted in its entirety in the present volume.)

Contributors

Barbara Nimri Aziz (Ph.D., School of Oriental and African Studies, University of London) is a research associate at the Center for the Study of Women and Society and the Department of Anthropology at City University of New York. She is author of *Tibetan Frontier Families: Reflections of Three Generations from Dingri* (New Delhi: Vikas, 1978); and co-editor (with Matthew Kapstein) of an interdisciplinary collection of articles in Tibetan studies, entitled *Soundings in Tibetan Civilization* (New Delhi: Manohar, 1985). She is currently preparing a book on contemporary Tibetan society.

Rita Gross (Ph.D., University of Chicago) is Associate Professor in the Department of Philosophy and Religious Studies at the University of Wisconsin, Eau Claire. Dr. Gross has authored numerous articles on women and religion. She coedited *Unspoken Worlds: Women's Religious Lives in Non-Western Cultures* (New York: Harper and Row, 1980, soon to appear in a second edition), and *Beyond Androcentrism: New Essays on Women and Religion*. Dr. Gross is a senior student of the late Chogyam Trungpa Rinpoche.

Janet Gyatso (Ph.D., University of California, Berkeley) is Assistant Professor of Religion at Amherst College. She has previously offered courses at SUNY (Stony Brook) and at Wesleyan University. Her dissertation studied the Tibetan visionary/engineer, Thang-stong rGyal-po. She has published a series of articles on the *gter-ma* tradition and related issues of authorship, revelation, memory and semiotics. She is working on a book about the sense of personal identity in the autobiographical reminiscences of 'Jigs-med Gling-pa, and is also studying the semiotics of the Buddhist mantra.

Miranda Shaw is a Ph.D. candidate at Harvard University who is working on a thesis on the *Cakrasaṁvara-tantra*. She has published articles on comparative philosophy and on women and the Tantras; and she has conducted research and translation efforts in India and Ladakh. Currently, she is translating works by female *siddhas*.

Karma Lekshe Tsomo received a Master's Degree in Asian Studies from the University of Hawaii in 1971 and studied for five years at the Library of Tibetan Works and Archives, Dharamsala. She received *śrāmaṇerikā* ordination in 1977, *bhikṣuni* ordination in 1982, and is currently studying at the Institute of Buddhist Dialectics in Dharamsala.

Janice D. Willis (Ph.D., Columbia University) is a full Professor of Religion at Wesleyan University, where she teaches Sanskrit and Tibetan Buddhism. In addition to a number of articles treating issues in Buddhist philosophy, women and Buddhism, and Buddhist biographical and hagiographical literature, her publications include *The Diamond Light; An Introduction to Tibetan Buddhist Meditations* (New York: Simon & Schuster 1972; rpt. 1973); *On Knowing Reality; The Tattvārtha Chapter of Asaṅga's Bodhisattvabhūmi* (New York: Columbia University Press, 1979; rpt. Delhi: Motilal Banarsidass, 1982); and *Enlightened Beings; Early dGe-lugs Siddha Biographies*, forthcoming from Wisdom Publications, London.